First Time Investor

Also by Gordon K. Williamson

Low Risk Investing

Making the Most of Your 401(k)

The 100 Best Mutual Funds You Can Buy, 2002

First Time Investor

by
Gordon K. Williamson

Adams Media Corporation
Holbrook, Massachusetts

Published by
Adams Media Corporation
260 Center Street, Holbrook, MA 02343 U.S.A.

ISBN: 1-58062-288-7

Printed in Canada.

J I H G F E D C B A

Library of Congress Cataloging-in-Publication Data
Williamson, Gordon K.
First Time Investor / Gordon K. Williamson.
p.   cm.
Includes index.
ISBN 1-58062-288-7
1. Investments. I. Title.
HG4521 .W4838   2001
332.6--dc21   2001022805

This publication is designed to provide accurate and authoritative information with regard to the subject matter covered. It is sold with the understanding that the publisher is not engaged in rendering legal, accounting, or other professional advice. If legal advice or other expert assistance is required, the services of a competent professional person should be sought.
— From a *Declaration of Principles* jointly adopted by a Committee of the American Bar Association and a Committee of Publishers and Associations

This book is available at quantity discounts for bulk purchases.
For information, call 1-800-872-5627.

Contents

Introduction

The underlying theme of this book is that most things in life, once stripped of their facade, folklore, confusion, and misperceptions, are not as difficult to understand as they seem—and that clear, demystified explanations of the basic concepts and principles at work will help you make smart decisions.

In the case of financial planning, it is important that first time investors understand the basic concepts and principles relating to the various instruments or categories of investment—from bank certificates of deposit (CDs) to foreign stocks, from money market and checking accounts to technology and gold mutual funds—before they begin to commit their savings to a particular investment. Once these basics are learned, investors will find they are able to make the simple decisions that will ensure their financial success.

This book explains and exposes the basic decisions investors must make—often between similar or complementary investments—and shows investors how to identify the right choices for their circumstances. The majority of people are either intimidated by investments, overcome with "information overload," or, frankly, bored with most investment advice. This book's goal is not to make you an expert but simply to make it easier for you to make the investment decisions you know you need to make, without dragging you through textbook explanations of all the quirks of every investment category.

One of the problems with most investment books is that they are written by either practitioners who have a hidden agenda (recommend investments that they specialize in, that pay high commissions, and so on) or academics who have no real-world experience. Fortunately for you, I deal in all types of investments, and my compensation is based on an annual fee. I do not have an ax to grind, and I do not have a particular type of investment to push. My goal is to help you make your financial decisions as insightful (and successful!) as possible.

CHAPTER 1

Getting Ready to
Get Started

Why the best time to invest is when you are ready

INVESTING BASICS

It may seem obvious that the best time to get started with any particular kind of
investment is as soon as you're ready, that is, when you feel fairly knowledgeable
about your chosen investment (you understand the potential return—and potential
losses—the tax ramifications, how it fits with the rest of your holdings, its long-
term historical record, and the length of time you will need to hold it). You should
not wait until you get some kind of confirming signal from your favorite financial
guru, a radio or television commentator, or an article in your favorite newspaper
or magazine.

Waiting until the stock market drops or rises 200 points, or for government
bond yields to climb or fall to 7.5%, or whatever signal you choose, is foolish.
First, the "signal" event might not take place for years—in the meantime, you'd
miss out on tremendous appreciation in your chosen investment. Second, there is
no guarantee that when a certain event, or series of events, does take place the
market is suddenly right for your investment. In fact, most investors who wait, for
example, for disaster to strike, change their minds once the anticipated event takes
place—adding another or a series of additional qualifications ("I'm going to wait
until the Dow drops another 200 points") and never get into the market at all.
There are two basic actions in investing: (1) actually committing your money and
(2) choosing an investment that is truly an investment as opposed to a gamble.

Committing Your Money

As basic as this qualification might sound, a number of armchair investors
track one or more securities on a daily basis, constantly muttering their regrets: "If

I had gone into this my money would have doubled by now," or "Thank goodness I am on the sidelines—because if I had gone into stocks last week I'd already be down $2,000."

The problem with this kind of "paper trading" is that your investment strategies are never tested by the real world—it's a little like reading a book about how to drive a racecar but never actually doing it. Tracking make-believe investments on paper means that you never actually lose money—and your mistakes don't really affect you. On the other hand, you're not going to make much money, either, if you're not playing with real money. It's not the real world! Paper trading is fine if you're interested in boasting to your friends or spouse about your magnificent investment track record. But if your goal is to make the most out of the money you have available for investments, you're going to need to make some serious choices—and actually put your money into the market.

Choosing the Right Investment

The second qualification is just as important. There are quite a few places that you can put your money that really should be considered gambling. Most option and commodity plays are simply bets. Buying penny stocks is another example. After all, there aren't many ways that you can really double your money in just a few days.

Each investment works differently, which is part of the beauty, and sometimes part of the confusion, of investing. In terms of making good choices, you can compare investing to choosing a car. Cars—just like investments—share a number of features; they have at least two seats, an engine, four wheels, doors, and so on.

But certain vehicles are designed for certain tasks, situations, or objectives. For example, a Chevrolet Corvette can hardly be considered a "family car." You probably don't think of a Toyota Corolla if you're looking for speed or sex appeal. Similarly, you should not invest in a limited partnership on a "whim" or for a short period—these investments are designed to be held for at least ten years and are difficult, if not impossible, to get out of early. Bank CDs may be a safe investment, but they're not a great choice if you're going to roll over the CD year after year, paying taxes along the way, plus putting your investment bankroll at the mercy of prevailing interest rates.

Once you understand the critical features of an investment—holding period, current income, volatility, appreciation potential, tax consequences, and so on—deciding whether or not it is a good choice for you becomes much easier. Furthermore, it is much less likely that you will make a poor choice or be taken advantage of if you know how the investment is supposed to work.

ADVANTAGES OF INVESTING

I believe there are several critical advantages to investing. Perhaps the greatest advantage is that, if things work out well, the investor can enjoy more leisure time, increase his or her comfort level, or provide more for his or her loved ones. Successful investing means increased freedom—freedom to perhaps move to a better neighborhood, start your own business, take an exotic trip, or get rid of nagging debts. Short-term, successful investing can make you feel great about yourself. Think how proud you would feel, at least for a couple of hours, if a stock you bought two weeks ago at $10 a share kept increasing in value and was now worth $14 a share.

DISADVANTAGES OF INVESTING

Unfortunately, most investments don't come with any kind of guarantee. Even investments backed by the U.S. government can fluctuate in value. Moreover, even if you hold an extremely secure investment until it matures, there is no guarantee that your purchasing power hasn't diminished by an even greater amount over the same period. And the more speculative investments, such as common stocks, can certainly drop in value, particularly if you only hold them for a short time.

Most investors protect themselves by diversifying their holdings, but well-diversified portfolios inevitably suffer from "envy." That is, for any given period, one category of investment—whether it's stocks or bonds or money market funds—will always outperform the others. Building a properly diversified investment portfolio guarantees that you'll wish in hindsight that you had invested more in what has turned out to be the winner for a particular quarter or year.

When all is said and done, however, consider the alternative to investing—not investing. By not doing anything productive with your money, by burying it in the proverbial tin can in the backyard or stuffing it under your mattress, you are not protecting your money or yourself. No matter where your money is, it is increasing or decreasing in value. Buried in your backyard, it is slowly being eaten up by the cumulative effects of inflation.

BUYING AND SELLING INVESTMENTS

It isn't hard to find reports of how an investment category has performed, but the information can be confusing or misleading. A number of financial publications such as *Money*, *Forbes*, *Fortune*, and *BusinessWeek* regularly publish performance figures, listing the best-performing stocks, bonds, and mutual funds.

What these charts, graphs, and ratings lack is historical perspective—as mutual funds point out in their advertisements, past performance is no guarantee of future results. Unfortunately, many investors read published performance results and believe they can expect similar results in the future.

These periodicals should include a warning along the lines of: "Caution—even though these results look great, keep in mind that the last ten years have been the best ever experienced by this investment category." Or, during a down period, something like: "Attention! Even though foreign securities have not done particularly well over the past three years when compared to U.S. stocks, this is not normal."

A General Rule

As a general rule, any given investment should comprise somewhere between 5% and 25% of your portfolio. The reason I suggest 5% as the low end is that a smaller percentage probably isn't worth the effort and expense—you'll see virtually no change in your net worth even if the investment experiences a terrific year. There is also the issue of keeping track of your holdings. Portfolios that are spread out among too many categories or securities often suffer from neglect.

The upper end of the suggested range, 25%, is somewhat arbitrary, just like the lower end of 5%. Nevertheless, the reason you should not make any single investment represent too large a portion of your portfolio is obvious—if such an investment declines precipitously, it will have a dramatic effect on your net worth; it could alter your lifestyle or force you to make changes in your investment plans that will hurt you in the long run.

Get Advice

There is no golden rule about the best way to buy or sell an investment. A number of publications will tell you that you can do it all on your own.

The truth is that with investing, you can do a number of things on your own—once you are thoroughly educated about how the investments you're considering work. But there are also a number of things you should only do with the help of professional counsel. Remember that investing seems easy when everything is going up in value; the situation becomes a lot more complicated—and riskier—when the market is fluctuating or heading downward or if you have suffered a series of losses.

The real question to ask yourself is whether or not an investment advisor can add value to your decision-making process. If he or she can, then the advisor is worth every penny he or she earns from the commission or management fee.

If there is no value added (for example, you already know you want to buy 100 shares of your favorite utility company and you can place the order through a discount brokerage firm), then paying a standard commission or fee is a waste of money. However, listening to additional advice can often be an invaluable learning experience. You may find an advisor who has a different approach to or perspective on investing, or perhaps someone who can point out or help you take advantage of opportunities you weren't even aware of.

RISK AND RETURN

The main risk of investing can be stated simply: *not getting what you expected*, which often happens when you invest in the more speculative kinds of investments. This can lead to an additional risk: *giving up on a category too quickly*. A disappointing month, quarter, year, or even couple of years may cause you to abandon an otherwise good investment category. Think about the number of people who invested in stocks just before the Crash of 1987. A good number of these people probably decided to get out—and stay out—of the stock market. The fact is that a fundamentally good investment category, whether it is bonds or small company stocks, will perform decently—but over time. The ingredient you need to add is *patience*.

There are also a couple of hidden risks to investing. First, do not minimize the effects of a loss. If an investment drops 25% in value, it must then appreciate 33% before you break even. (If a stock drops from 10 to 7½, it has dropped 25% of its value. To rise from 7½ to 10, it must gain 33%—the same dollar amount, but a significantly greater percentage gain.)

Second, a number of your most conservative investments can turn out to be quite risky during inflationary times—if risk is properly calculated to include your diminishing purchasing power.

TAX CONSIDERATIONS

One of the most important issues you'll face in making investment decisions will be the tax consequences of your actions. As a former tax attorney and the first author to ever write about the tax efficiency of mutual funds, I feel that I can shed some light on this often confusing subject.

In recent years, the importance of the tax consequences of an investment has been blown out of proportion. Investors suddenly become angry when they discover how much they're going to have to pay in taxes because their broker was a successful trader. Again, consider the alternative: If you made little or no money, the tax consequences would be negligible. Personally, I don't know of anyone who wants to be below the poverty level so that he or she won't have to pay taxes. Until the top marginal bracket becomes 100% (in some countries, the luxury tax on certain items is over 100%), don't get upset about the effect your success will have on your tax bracket. Our tax system—as confusing and unfair as it might seem—is still better for investors than those of a lot of other countries.

The tax consequences often blind people to the actual performance of an investment. If you doubt what I say, consider the hundreds of billions of dollars invested in what turned out to be worthless partnerships and other tax-motivated ventures. In such cases, the investor would have been better off by putting his or her money into an investment category that was fully taxable each year.

Whether an investment is tax-friendly or not should be taken seriously, but it should not be at the top of your list of investing criteria. Before looking at an investment's potential for taxation, first ask yourself whether the investment is a good choice considering your time horizon, risk level, and other holdings.

Until the gap between ordinary income tax and capital gains taxes becomes wider, investing inside a qualified retirement account such as an IRA, 401(k), or profit-sharing plan remains a better choice for most investors planning for their retirement. Tax-deferred growth is always preferable to current taxation.

Even if income tax rates increase in the future (which is unlikely given the political environment surrounding taxation), you're better off deferring taxes on your investments as long as you're going to be able to give the investment at least a few years of deferred growth.

IS INVESTING RIGHT FOR YOU?

As the author of over 30 books on investing, I am certainly biased in its favor. Even from an objective perspective, I believe one would have to say that through investing, at the very least, you can increase your knowledge of the world and the way it works, you can experience certain unique emotions (sometimes pleasant ones!), and you'll always have an endlessly fascinating topic of conversation at hand.

Young and old alike can profit from investing. It can benefit the rich as well as the poor. Successful investing is one of the few ways that a person with a moderate income can end up being wealthy.

Surprisingly, successful investing is not solely about producing great returns. For example, you might be able to double your net worth, but end up with an ulcer or a divorce in the process. Success, in most cases, is the result of regularly adding new money to your investments or reinvesting dividends or interest. Well over 90 percent of the people I know who I would classify as "financially wealthy" were tortoiselike in their approach—investing a few dollars whenever possible—always looking at the finish line instead of what was around the next bend.

Successful investing doesn't guarantee happiness, but when things are going well with your portfolio, few things feel as good. And, as mentioned earlier, investing can increase your freedom. You can use successful investing to open doors for yourself that would have been unattainable otherwise—from retiring early, to starting your own business, to just taking advantage of the opportunity to do something you've always wanted to do.

CHAPTER 2

Certificates of Deposit

*The advantages and disadvantages of placing
your savings in "safe and secure" bank CDs*

BANK CD BASICS

Are banks still a good place to put your money? For those most conservative with
their money, a savings account at the local bank might represent at least a secure
haven. And as more and more banks have merged or consolidated operations, one
might expect that depositors would somehow benefit from the increased efficiency these bigger banks enjoy. What has happened instead is that banks and savings and loan associations are now charging fees for services that, until a few
years ago, were free. Moreover, charges for services that have traditionally cost
something have also been increasing.

According to more than one national publication, the average bank account
can expect to pay over $120 a year in fees (for example, monthly checking fees,
automated teller charges). With the imposition of a fee to talk to a teller now at
some banks, a comedian recently pointed out that one prominent bank was going
to charge you $2 every time you even thought about your checking account.

When you deposit money in a bank or savings and loan association, you are,
in essence, lending them your money. In return for the use of your money, the
financial institution loans out or invests your money at a higher rate. If they are
offering you a rate of return that is X, then they are taking your money and getting X plus Y with it. The difference, or spread, compensates the bank for any risk
it may take when lending your money out or investing it elsewhere, pays for overhead, and provides the bank with a profit.

In most cases, when you invest your money you will not have any guarantees; your money will be at risk. By putting your money in a savings account you

are letting the bank or financial institution accept these risks for you. Therefore you will receive a lower rate of return. But banks do offer a kind of deposit account that provides a better return without exposing you to risk.

What Are CDs?

Certificates of deposit, more commonly referred to as CDs, represent a type of deposit with a bank or savings and loan association. The depositor (investor) agrees to deposit his or her money with a financial institution in return for receiving a set rate of return. The yield, or return, depends upon the amount of money being deposited, the term of the deposit, the general level of interest rates, and the competitiveness of the institution. At the end of the term, the lender (you) is free either to liquidate the entire account, principal, and accumulated interest, or to roll the maturing CD over into another CD for another term. The renewal rate may be higher, lower, or identical to the previous rate.

ADVANTAGES OF CDS

Whenever one thinks of bank CDs, the first things that come to mind are safety and a known rate of return. When the bank offers you a certain rate of return, you get that rate, no matter what happens to the bank's investment portfolio, the economy, or your specific dollars. This simplicity is one of the major attractions of CDs. If you do not like the rate of return being offered, you are always free to shop elsewhere, getting quotes and yields from other banks or savings and loan associations.

DISADVANTAGES OF CDS

There are two possible disadvantages to investing your money in CDs. First, if you make a withdrawal before the CD matures, you could pay a penalty. The amount of penalty depends upon the CDs interest rate and the financial institution. The second potential disadvantage could end up being a positive rather than a negative. That is, when you lock into a certain rate of return, you will only know after the fact if this was a better way to go than opting for something that had a floating rate, such as a money market account or an adjustable-rate mortgage fund.

There is a way to partially or fully avoid both of these possible situations: staggering the maturity of your CDs. For example, if you have $40,000 to invest, it may be best to equally divide the money and invest in four different CDs that have different maturity dates (for example, three months, six months, one year, and two years). When the three-month CD matures, roll it over into a six-month CD if cash is not needed at that time (your existing six-month CD will have only three more months until maturity at this point). Staggered maturities may increase your bookkeeping efforts, and the rate of return could very well be different for each CD, but this minimizes your chances of facing a penalty since money is maturing every few months.

In theory, there is also a distant chance that your financial institution will run into trouble. Therefore, when you invest in a CD, make sure it is backed by the Federal Deposit Insurance Corporation (FDIC). Furthermore, do not invest more than $90,000 with any one institution. That way, in case there is an insolvency, reorganization, or FDIC takeover, your account is protected for up to $100,000 (your $90,000 of principal plus accumulated interest—which is why you do not want to invest $100,000).

RISK AND RETURN

Until the late 1970s and early 1980s, the rates of return in CDs were not particularly competitive with other investments. With the introduction of money market accounts and the resulting exodus out of CDs into these more appealing accounts, banks wised up and began offering rates that were very similar to the more liquid money market funds.

Over the past decade, CD rates have followed the general trend and performance of other short-term instruments. Usually offering a somewhat lower rate in return for absolute safety and investor familiarity, they remained an extremely popular investment. Even during the early 1990s, when rates fell to the 3% to 4% range, hundreds of billions of dollars were still in CDs.

TAX CONSIDERATIONS

The interest or yield of CDs is fully taxable on a local, state, and federal basis (few localities impose a city or county income tax). At the end of each year, your financial institution will send you a 1099 form, indicating how much interest has been earned in your account. You must claim this entire dollar figure on your tax return.

Like general-purpose money market funds, the only way to avoid current taxation with CDs is if they are part of a qualified retirement plan (IRA, pension plan, and so on). For nonretirement accounts, the fact that you didn't receive or ever see the accumulated interest is unimportant. Automatic reinvestment plans or CDs that roll over at maturity do not escape current taxation.

BUYING AND SELLING CDS

The best way to buy CDs is by making a few telephone calls. Find out what bank or savings and loan association near you is offering the best rates and any "convenience features" they offer. These features may include free services or the ability to add to or withdraw a certain dollar amount once or twice during the term of the CD.

Convenience is a very important consideration. If you have $10,000 that you have earmarked for CDs, and an institution near you offers, say, 5%, whereas another bank across town guarantees 5.2% for the year, you have to ask yourself if it's worth your time to spend an hour in the car, back and forth, to get an extra $20 for the year (perhaps only $14 on an after-tax basis).

CDs have no secondary marketplace. If you wish to sell your CD at or prior to maturity, contact your financial institution and give them liquidation instructions. You may decide that you need access to part or all of the money. Whatever the case, find out how much money can be sent to you or delivered elsewhere, or if it is necessary for you to make the withdrawal in person. Make sure that you find out whether there are any penalties or costs involved. Weigh such costs, if any, against the benefit of any alternative investment. If the money is being used for an important purchase, this may be a moot point.

There are three ways to see how you are doing. First, you can contact the bank or savings and loan association to find out your current balance. Second, you can rely on their monthly or quarterly statements. Third, your newspaper may include a financial section that lists CD rates from around the country.

Although not previously described, there is another type of CD worth considering, the "brokered CD." Brokered CDs have the following features: (1) they are bought and sold through brokerage firms, (2) there is an active secondary marketplace for purchasers and sellers, (3) there are FDIC insured up to $100,000, (4) there is no prepayment penalty if sold prior to maturity, (5) they can be sold prior to maturity, subject to "market adjustment," (6) a premature sale would result in an additional profit to the investor if rates were lower at the time of the sale than they were when the CD was first purchased (or loss of some principle if the interest rates were *higher* at the time of the sale), and (7) interest is credited to the account on a regular basis and any premature seller is still entitled to all accrued interest.

Brokered CDs will often be the favored choice for any CD investor because of the features described above plus the fact that the brokerage firm you are dealing with will most likely have access to CDs from around the country. This greater access to banks across the nation should result in a higher yield to the investor plus the convenience of having all security and CD positions held at one institution. When the brokered CD matures or it is sold prematurely, proceeds will automatically go into an interest-bearing money market account.

ARE CDS RIGHT FOR YOU?

Bank CDs are an adequate choice for the ultraconservative retirement plan participant who doesn't ever want to see a decline in value on his or her statement but understands that, on an after-inflation basis (and the eventual taxation when the retirement account is liquidated), this is not a good choice. If you are determined to include certificates of deposit as part of your overall holdings, then a qualified retirement plan such as a 401(k) is the place for this investment, because you will be sheltered from current income taxes (and 100% of the return of a CD is normally subject to income taxes each year).

As one of America's most popular investments, it is difficult to say that CDs are something that should not be included in a portfolio. Yet, for most people, there are better alternatives. During periods when interest rates are rising, money market funds are a better choice (no penalties and your rate of return will go up as the general level of rates also increases). When interest rates seem to be stable, or even dropping, then short-term bond funds are a better choice. Their return is often several percentage points higher than that offered by CDs, and again, there is no penalty for a "premature" withdrawal.

Nevertheless, you may still find CDs appealing for a couple of reasons. First, you know up front what you will end up with and what it will cost to take money out early. Second, since the deposit is usually local, there is a certain amount of psychological sense of safety. Third, this will always be an investment that is familiar to most investors and easy to understand.

By the time you have finished reading this book, your need or desire to invest in CDs will be greatly diminished. Once you have learned about all the other alternatives, you will find it necessary to keep little, if any, money in CDs.

CHAPTER 3

Money Market Funds

*Why money market mutual funds are
a better choice for your savings than bank CDs*

MONEY MARKET FUND BASICS

As we saw last chapter, bank CDs offer the ultraconservative investor a guaranteed rate of return in exchange for very few, if any, investment bells and whistles. But you may ask yourself, "Is there a better alternative to a traditional bank account, and if so, where do I find it?" Fortunately, you do have an alternative: a money market account as offered by banks, brokerage firms, or mutual fund companies.

Money market funds were introduced in this country in the early 1970s. They are a type of mutual fund that invests in short-term debt instruments, such as U.S. Treasury bills, CDs, Eurodollar CDs, and commercial paper. In order to be called a "money market" fund, at least 95% of the fund's assets must be invested in securities that are rated extremely safe. The typical maturity of the average money market fund fluctuates from 25 to 65 days; each portfolio has some securities maturing within a few days, weeks, and months. As the "paper" matures, fund managers reinvest it in other short-term instruments immediately. No money market manager wants portfolio money sitting around idly, even for a day.

The rate of return for money market funds has consistently been higher than that offered by U.S. Treasury bills and interest-bearing checking and savings accounts. Usually, money market funds have also had yields that have surpassed those offered by short-term CDs. Like interest rates in general, the return that money market funds have provided has been all over the board in the past 20 years, ranging anywhere from just under 4% in the early 1990s to near 20% during the very early 1980s.

When you invest in a money market fund, your money is commingling with everyone else's. Each investor, whether seasoned or new, gets the same yield. If the quoted yield is, say, 5.20%, you will get that rate, just like an investor who has been with the fund for several years (and got a much higher rate years earlier).

For example, let's suppose you invested $4,000 in a money market fund and your order was received by the fund tomorrow. At the same time the order is placed by the broker, other orders from around the country are also being processed. The fund manager adds up the value of all these checks and buys money market instruments, as described in the prospectus. If rates are moving upward, the existing yield of 5.20% may go up to 5.23% due to the "new" money going out and buying very short-term bonds, CDs, and so forth, that had a yield of 5.5%. The reason the entire portfolio would not go up very much on any given day or week is that new monies (or existing paper in the portfolio that has just matured) represent an extremely small portion of the total assets (that is, a $2 billion money market fund with a current yield of 5.37% is largely unaffected if $700,000 comes in one day and is invested at 5.44%). However, over several days and weeks, if the general level of short-term interest rates is changing, all money market funds will gradually reflect those newer rates.

ADVANTAGES OF MONEY MARKET FUNDS

There are many advantages to owning money market funds. First of all, money market accounts are safe and secure. Just like T-bills or bank CDs, there really is no risk associated with money market funds. True, in theory, there could be moderate or massive defaults within the fund's portfolio, but this is not likely when one considers the incredible safety record of these instruments and the fact that their quality is regulated by the Securities Exchange Commission. Only one such fund, set up by bankers for bankers, has lost money.

In addition to being extremely safe, the rate of return stays competitive with the general level of interest rates; as rates climb, so do money market yields and vice versa.

The mutual fund industry is highly competitive. There are literally hundreds and hundreds of money market accounts that want your money. These funds know that the best way to get your money is to offer you the highest yield possible. Such yields are quoted on a regular basis in monthly financial magazines and on an annual basis in such books as *The 100 Best Mutual Funds You Can Buy* (updated annually by yours truly).

These funds are extremely liquid and marketable, and the firms that offer money market accounts emphasize customer service. Money can be added or taken out at any time. You can use your telephone and request that a certain dollar amount be sent to you immediately (some funds require that this request be made in writing). You may be able to structure your fund so that money can automatically be wired to or from an account. Or you can set up most money market accounts so that one or more of your bills (for example, rent, mortgage, car payment, student loan) are automatically paid each month. This program, known as a systematic withdrawal plan (SWP), is a means to provide you, or a creditor, with a specific dollar amount each month.

Those money market funds offered by brokerage firms and mutual fund groups also give you quite a bit of investment flexibility. With a phone call to the mutual fund family, you can tell them to liquidate part or all of the ABC money market fund and have it transferred the same day into the ABC stock fund or ABC bond fund. These investment options allow you to respond quickly to market conditions, without the hassle and delay of waiting for a check and filling out an application or seeing a broker in person.

Most money market funds include check-writing privileges. Mutual funds and brokerage firms let you write as many checks as you want without cost, service fee, or monthly charge; even the checks are free—when you start to run out you can reorder more checks, again for free. Usually there is a minimum dollar figure that the check can be written for; it is quite common to see a money market check that is imprinted with the following: "This check must be for at least $250." This high minimum per check cuts down on the number of checks written by shareholders. Reduced transaction costs are passed on to the investor in the form of a higher yield. Some brokerage firms, banks, and so forth have no minimum amount that they will accept, but charge a nominal fee for each check written. A number of funds also offer a credit or debit card.

DISADVANTAGES OF MONEY MARKET FUNDS

There are only two disadvantages to money market funds: (1) the process of "banking by mail" and (2) the variability of the rate of return.

The majority of money market funds offered by brokerage firms and mutual fund companies have check-writing minimums, which may or may not fit your needs. Further, you still need some place you can cash a check when you need money; this may not be so easy, even if you are near a branch office of your brokerage firm or mutual fund company. Finally, unless you deal with a local branch office, deposits are done through the mail. This means that you will not earn interest on such deposits until the money market institution receives them.

Assuming it takes three days for the mail, the yield on such an account is 5.5%, and deposits total $20,000 a year; this comes out to less than $11 a year.

RISK AND RETURN

As already described, the rate of return rises and falls with the general trend of interest rates. At first, most investors prefer to lock in a rate of return. However, once it is explained to them that this is not the most conservative approach, they often change their mind.

The reason a guaranteed rate of return should usually be avoided is interest rates go up and down. When you are offered a certain rate of return, you will know only in hindsight if your return was good in light of interim changes with interest rates and inflation. A set rate of return ends up being beneficial only if interest rates, during the time of ownership, end up staying the same or, better yet, decline. If rates instead go up, then a floating rate would have been better.

BUYING AND SELLING MONEY MARKET FUNDS

Mutual funds, banks, savings and loan associations, credit unions, and brokerage firms all offer money market accounts. All money market funds are bought and sold for $1 a share. Interest in your account is credited in the form of additional shares. You may have 4,000 shares one day (representing exactly $4,000) and 4,000.61 a day later (the .61 share represents interest for one day). Your money goes to work for you the same day it is received by the mutual fund company. Most money market funds have to be established with at least $1,000. Funds will not close down the account if your balance later falls below the initial minimum.

Since the price per share remains at a constant $1, the only thing to track is current yield (return). A large number of newspapers have financial sections that list representative samples of the rates of returns of several investments, including bank CDs, T-bills, government bonds, and money market accounts.

If you want to find out what your account has been earning over some past period, or simply wish to find out what the current rate of return is, you can contact the person who sold you the fund or telephone the fund directly. Virtually all money market funds have toll-free telephone numbers. You can use their automated quotation system 24 hours a day or speak directly to an account representative during normal business hours.

TAX CONSIDERATIONS

There are three categories of money market funds: general purpose, government backed, and tax-free. Each category is taxed differently. The majority of money market accounts come under the heading "general purpose." These funds comprise instruments that are fully taxable on a federal and state level (assuming you live in a state that has an income tax).

A small number of funds consist solely of T-bills or seasoned government obligations that mature within a year. Since direct obligations of the U.S. government are exempt from state and local income taxes, these funds enjoy the same tax-exempt status. But even though this category of money market funds is fully loaded with government paper, it is fully taxable for federal income tax purposes. These funds can be easily identified by their title.

A fair number of money market funds comprise municipal obligations that mature in a year or less and are exempt from federal income taxes. Furthermore, no state or local income taxes are due on the interest if you invest in a money market fund comprised of tax-free notes issued in your state of residency or live in a state that has no income tax.

If you overreact to financial events over some given period, you can always seek out money market funds that are invested entirely in government-backed paper. Your yield will not be quite as high as a traditional, or common purpose, money fund, but you will gain that needed peace of mind.

ARE MONEY MARKET FUNDS RIGHT FOR YOU?

As odd as it might sound, for the very conservative investor, a money market fund is probably a better choice than a bank CD since money market accounts have a variable rate that often changes daily. A CD investor who locks in a certain rate of return for a set period, ranging from several days to ten years, is almost betting that interest rates are going to do X (for example, if you thought rates were going to go down, you would lock into a long-term CD and preserve a high rate of return for the term of the CD; if you thought rates were headed upward, you would stick with short-term CDs, thinking that you would continuously roll over the CD as it matured into a higher-yielding CD). With a money market fund, there is no need to "bet." If rates do go up, a money market fund will start to yield more; if rates decline, the same fund will slowly lower its return.

Money market funds are the perfect place to invest a large portion of the money you want to keep liquid. This is also a good "safe haven" to park your assets during periods of economic uncertainty or disaster.

Everyone should have part of his or her portfolio in a money market fund, if for no other reason than to be able to get your hands on cash in a hurry. Not only does this give one peace of mind, it's also a good source to tap when it comes time to pay monthly bills and for emergencies.

Several financial writers suggest that you should have between six months and a year's worth of salary or income tied up in a money market fund. These writers somehow believe that other parts of a portfolio—stocks, bonds, bank CDs, and mutual funds—are not "liquid." Your decision as to how much of your portfolio should be invested in a money market fund should depend upon such things as (1) whether you are anticipating a large purchase, such as an automobile, during the coming year; (2) the security of your job and/or that of your spouse; (3) major lifestyle changes that may be on the horizon (for example, having a baby, remodeling the home, going back to school, going through a divorce, moving); and (4) whether you have a negative outlook about real estate, stocks, and/or bonds.

Money market funds are a lot like vanilla ice cream: nice, predictable, safe, unexciting. This category of investments is not given much attention or lip service by brokers or advisors since it is one of the most basic, and boring, investments. Yet, part of our holdings should be in something that is not exciting—something we can count on whether or not there is world tension, a stock market crash, chaos in the bond market, or a depression in real estate.

CHAPTER 4

Stocks

Why—despite the dramatic ups and downs of the stock market—
common stocks are the *choice for all but the most conservative investor*

STOCK BASICS

Wouldn't it be nice to own General Motors, IBM, Sony, DaimlerChrysler, DuPont, or Microsoft? Well, when you buy the common stock of one of these companies, you become an owner. And, like any other business, some years are better than others. But, as a business owner, you begin to realize that it is important to be patient.

It is extremely doubtful that the founder and head of Microsoft, Bill Gates, sees his stock drop in value one month, quarter, year, or even a couple of years in a row and says, "Gee, maybe this company isn't so good after all. Maybe I should sell all of my stock and put the money in the bank." When described in this context, the worrying that stock owners do seems rather silly.

A Comparison

Let's look at common stocks in another context: compared to residential real estate.

If you bought a home in the early 1980s, there is a strong likelihood that it is now worth more than what you paid for it. However, for a time at the end of that decade and well into the 1990s you would have seen the value of your home drop. According to the National Association of Realtors, it takes five years to break even on a home—assuming an average performing market. Those years for real estate were certainly not "average"; prices in most parts of the country fell anywhere from 10% to 60%. Some of the more extreme examples could be found in California, particularly with homes in the $500,000 to $2 million range.

Assume you bought a home for $200,000 in 1988, and by 1995 it was worth $170,000. You might have thought that it was "only" a 15% loss ($30,000 divided by $200,000). However, if you are like most people, you didn't buy the home for cash; instead, you made a down payment and took out a mortgage. This means that if you put down $40,000 (20% down), you actually suffered a 75% loss ($30,000 divided by $40,000) because three-fourths of your principal was lost. Yet, even with such a loss, you were probably not going to sell your house and declare, "I'm never buying another piece of real estate!" The point is that though stocks too have their volatile ups and downs, it would be extremely rare to experience a 75% loss with a well-diversified stock portfolio.

What Are Stocks?

Common stocks represent an ownership interest in a corporation. A corporation has two ways to raise money: by borrowing or by selling an interest or partial ownership in the business to people. Corporations borrow money from financial institutions or by issuing bonds. Ownership interests are sold by issuing stock.

If the existing owners of a corporation decide to "go public," this means that they are willing to sell part of the business in return for cash. The sale is made to the public via underwriters and institutional bankers who help structure the stock offering (the price per share, the number of shares to be issued, what brokerage firms will be involved in the sale of the securities, and so on). A corporation that has already issued shares in the past is considered to be a "public company," since part, most, or all of the ownership is now in the hands of the shareholders. Such a business has already gone public, but usually still can issue additional shares of stock to raise more capital. An example may help you better understand the concept of ownership.

Your Corporation

Suppose you own a corporation with three other friends. The four of you decided that you wanted to expand your operations and needed to raise quite a bit of money. You do not want to borrow the money because servicing such a debt, either by paying interest on bonds or from a bank loan, would increase your costs of doing business. Instead, you agree to sell off, say, 60% of the business in return for more working capital. After making some contacts and having some appraisals done, it is discovered that your corporation has a market value of $10 million.

By selling off 60%, you expect to raise somewhere around $6 million (60% of the company's worth), minus underwriting, legal, accounting, and other costs. Investment bankers structure the deal so that a total of 600,000 shares will be offered at $10 per share. If all the shares are sold and $6 million is raised, you will still own 10% of a business that has a market value of $10 million. Each of your three partners will also own 10% of the business. The corporation's value is based on the total market value of its stock, minus any liabilities.

The example makes it sound easy to raise money—but it isn't. First, you must have a group of investment bankers and underwriters who believe that your business is worth X amount of dollars and are willing to help you sell off a small, moderate, or large percentage of the business to the public. The "public" could end up being mutual funds, pension plans, money managers, individual investors, brokerage firms, or anyone else who believes in the future of the corporation.

The fact that you and a group of organizers want to sell shares of stocks does not mean that anyone is going to buy into the company. The marketplace (the public) may feel the price per share is too high, the future prospects for the business are not good, or a new offering is not a good idea in light of recent market or economic news. On the other hand, people may be very excited about your product or service and believe that you are the next Apple Computer, GM, or McDonald's. Gauging what the price per share should be and the number of shares that should be issued—in short, the value of the business—is determined by the investment bankers. They usually have a pretty good pulse on what's good or bad and what the marketplace is looking for and its current mood.

Once a company has gone public, it can issue additional shares of stock at any time in the future, as outlined by its corporate charter. The corporate charter can be amended or changed with the requisite number of votes from the share-holders—the people or entities that now own the company. Any such shares issued in the future can be easily priced since one share is worth just as much as any other share, and therefore new shares would be based on the market price of the shares currently trading.

Your Share of the Corporation

Stocks are special because they offer you a chance to own part of almost any publicly traded company you like. The number of shares you own is limited to the size of your pocketbook. If the company does well, so will you. And although an increasingly profitable company doesn't assure you of making huge stock profits, there is a strong relationship between the sales or revenues of a company and its price per share. There are a lot of great corporations that you and I will never be able to own, but we can be partial owners by buying their stock. When you own individual stocks, you receive annual reports from each company you "partially own."

Common stocks represent the easiest and perhaps the only long-term sure way of making real money. It's also easy to lose money in stocks. There's no one forcing you to hold onto a stock after it has dropped in value or stopping you from loading up on a "sure thing." The power of greed and fear is almost unlimited. This is one of the few investments in this book where it is possible to see substantial percentage drops in value unless there is diversification and patience. On the positive side, common stocks are the only inflation-hedge investment that goes up most years and has consistently been a winner.

Additional Caveats

Perhaps the most unique thing about stocks is the amount of misinformation and wrong opinions that can be found floating around them. When stock prices are high, people say that there is going to be a crash or sudden drop known as a "correction." When there is a crash or drop, these same people say that it is going to get even worse. Never lose sight of the fact that newspapers, magazines, and radio and television shows that report the news are in a business. Their business is market share. Each of these sources is competing with the others to get more listeners, readers, or viewers. Good news has never sold; bad news and disasters always create interest. One of the more harmful things to the stock market is the news media. The flow of information is critical to our freedom, well-being, and business, but distorted news can be harmful, turning people off to what has and continues to be absolutely the best investment— American (and foreign) enterprise.

ADVANTAGES OF OWNING STOCKS

There are two advantages to owning common stocks: appreciation potential and dividend income. Most people buy stocks for growth; they hope that they can buy shares for X dollars per share and later sell these same shares for X plus Y. If you're lucky and have picked the right company, the stock may go up quite a bit—leaving you with a significant profit. Historically, stocks have been one of the best hedges against inflation.

When a publicly traded corporation makes a profit, it can either pay out part or most of that profit in the form of a dividend to its shareholders, or retain the money for internal growth (more advertising, increased production, greater research and development, the buying of other businesses, and so on). The corporation's board of directors determines what should be done with corporate profits. These board members are elected by the shareholders.

DISADVANTAGES OF OWNING STOCKS

There are three disadvantages to owning common stocks: (1) Your principal can be lost if the price per share declines; (2) there is no guarantee that a company will pay a dividend, maintain its current dividend, or later increase its dividend; (3) the decision to buy or sell the stock is frequently based on irrationality.

When people buy stock, they do so because they feel the price per share will go up. The chance of losing money is not seriously considered. Hundreds of millions of dollars are made and lost each day in the stock market. Fortunately, if a stock drops in price, the loss is only a "paper loss" until the shares are actually sold. Similarly, if the price per share rises from what you paid, the profit is also only on paper. You don't actually make or lose any money from price increases or decreases until you sell part or all of your shares.

No matter how bright the future may look for a company, things can change. Critical managers can quit, die, or be replaced. Market share can change because of a competitive new product or an innovative advertising campaign. If earnings reports are disappointing, the price of the stock will almost certainly begin to slide. And the fact that you bought the stock at its "52-week low" doesn't mean that it won't hit a new low tomorrow, next week, next month, or next year.

A company that has a history of paying dividends, perhaps even increasing dividends over the years, will probably continue to do so, but you have no recourse if the board of directors decides to either suspend or cut down the dividend. Stock dividends are not like bond interest payments, which are guaranteed by the issuing corporation.

Owning stock can be a very emotional experience—with major-league ups and downs. People choose specific investments for a lot of different reasons: out of fear (putting money in CDs and money market accounts for safety), hope (saving enough in mutual funds to buy a house, pay for a college education, or retire), or greed (hoping the investment will double in value in a couple of months). For these reasons, most people end up buying at market highs and selling at market lows—they see how much money investors have made in stocks and want their share, or they're worried about getting out before they lose everything they own! Everyone likes to buy clothes and cars on sale, but no one seems to like to buy stocks or bonds when they are "on sale."

Also, the problem of properly evaluating stocks can give small investors major headaches. Annual reports tend to be extremely optimistic. Not being able to read between the lines could give you a false sense of security.

RISK AND RETURN

The track record for common stocks as a whole has been excellent. This investment has outperformed real estate, bonds, bank CDs, art, rare coins, oil, gold, and any other investment you can think of. Long-term, common stocks have been the best-performing investment category, and the future looks even brighter than the past. There is not a person alive who hasn't seen the market go up during his or her lifetime (unless he or she was born in the year 2000). No matter if you're four years old or 100 years old, the market is higher today than it was when you were born. This is not true with most other investments. Think about it. Gold is trading at half of its early 1980s high; silver is trading at less than one-tenth of its high; real estate prices have just recently seen their pre-1989 highs for several years (many areas of the country have had depressed real estate prices for over a decade, until late 1996); bond and CD yields are a fraction of what they were 20 years ago; and art, oil, and rare coin prices have collapsed. Yet, stock prices continue to increase almost every year (as do corporate profits and scales of efficiency).

As previously mentioned, some stocks pay dividends and others do not. The fact that a corporation pays a dividend does not mean that it is a good or bad stock. In the past, some of the best performing equities (stocks) have been those that paid an attractive dividend, whereas other top performers have never paid a dividend. In general, the greater the dividend, the less risk there is (and presumably the less reward). This is because a dividend payment can help partially or fully offset a depressed stock price. If you own shares of a company that pays a 4% dividend and the stock drops 10% during the year, your real loss is only 6%. However, if the same stock drop occurred with a company that paid no dividend, the loss would be exactly 10% (for example, you paid $10 a share for XYZ stock, and it is now worth $9 a share).

In a strange sense, there are two risks to stocks: owning them and not owning them. We have all heard about the risks of owning stocks, but few people talk about the risk of not owning stock. You want to own stocks not because they are fun and exciting, but because the price of goods and services goes up each year, and few investments are a good hedge against inflation.

When you buy a stock (or a mutual fund or variable annuity that invests in common stocks), there is no guarantee that it will go up in price. You can get a good idea as to how volatile the stock might be by asking the broker the stock's 52-week high and low price (for example, a stock that has a 52-week range of 20 to 46 is generally riskier than one that has a range of 10 to 14). This will show you the top and bottom price paid for the stock over the previous year. Of course, there is no assurance that the stock will not sell for more than the previous high or less than its low for the year.

BUYING AND SELLING STOCK

You cannot buy shares of a company unless someone is willing to sell them to you. Similarly, once you own shares, they can be sold only if there is a buyer.

In the case of most stocks, there is an active market and shares are traded by the thousands or tens of thousands Monday through Friday. Where the shares are traded depends on where the stock is listed. The biggest stock exchange is the New York Stock Exchange (NYSE), which accounts for about 75% of all exchange activity. The American Stock Exchange (AMEX) accounts for close to a fifth of the activity, and the remaining regional exchanges, located in places like San Francisco and Boston, account for the balance. Several thousand stocks are not traded on a formal exchange but instead are bought and sold "over-the-counter" (a network of market makers). This system, referred to as the OTC market, is largely computerized by a sophisticated network known as NASDAQ. All stocks traded on a formal exchange or NASDAQ are easily tracked through stock retrieval systems or software programs that use a telephone modem, cable, satellite dish, or FM reception for updates.

If you have an account at a securities firm, you can simply telephone in a buy or a sell order for individual securities. If you work through a broker who knows you, you may be able to make purchases even though there's no money in your account. When this happens, you have up to three business days to pay for the transaction. This is true whether or not you are buying stocks, bonds, or shares of a mutual fund. Similarly, you can sell your securities even though you—and not the broker—have physical possession of the certificate; you must bring in or send in the certificate within three business days.

If the three-day rule is not met, the brokerage firm can give you an extension of a few more days. If the trade is not settled by that time (meaning you have not come up with the cash or delivered the securities), the firm will be forced to "sell you out" (reverse the trade) and bill you for any losses, fees, or commissions.

When you own shares of individual securities, you decide when to sell them. At the time of purchase, or later, you can request that the certificate remain at the brokerage firm (a situation referred to as being held in "street name") or be sent to you. In most cases, it is best to have the certificate held by the brokerage firm. This makes any subsequent sale much easier. If the brokerage firm holds the certificates, dividends, capital gains, and/or interest payments can be automatically reinvested or placed directly into a money market fund.

Stock Prices

There are two prices for every stock: the bid price and the ask price. The bid price represents what you would get for the stock if you had shares to sell.

The ask price is the price you would pay if you wanted to buy shares. The ask price is always higher than the bid price. The difference between the bid and ask price is also known as the "spread." This spread or difference is what the market maker keeps as a profit. The market maker is the person who inventories the stock on the exchange and is who your broker or brokerage firm would go to if shares were being bought or sold. Every stock has a market maker. This person stands ready to buy or sell shares. Market makers play an important role in the stock market because they can help stabilize prices during periods of panic.

The difference between the bid and ask price is normally 12.5 cents ($\frac{1}{8}$ of a point) for widely traded stocks such as GM, IBM, McDonald's, and so forth. For less frequently traded stocks, the spread is usually 25 cents per share ($\frac{1}{4}$ of a point). The greater the spread between the bid and ask price, the greater the likelihood that the stock is not particularly popular or widely traded. Thus, when you see a bid–ask spread of $\frac{1}{2}$ point (50 cents per share) or more, this should tell you that it is a "thinly traded" stock and is therefore probably quite volatile (risky) and may be difficult to sell if the price were to collapse. A large spread between the bid and ask price does not benefit the buyer, seller, broker, or brokerage firm. In fact, it may not even benefit the market maker since his or her inventory of the stock is more at risk due to wide price movements.

Common stock prices are found every day in your local newspaper, the *Wall Street Journal*, and *Investor's Daily*, and weekly in *Barron's*. Full-service and discount brokerage firms can be contacted during their normal business hours for telephone quotes. You can also directly subscribe to a quotation service at home or at work if you have a computer and modem or FM receiver.

Selecting Stocks for Your Portfolio

Hundreds of books have been written outlining different strategies for picking stocks. However, there are a few basics you should keep in mind.

If an investor is in need of current income, he or she will normally be attracted to high-dividend-paying stocks. The term high-dividend-paying is relative and depends upon what percentage other investments are yielding. A 4% dividend looks attractive if bank CDs or money market accounts are paying only 4% to 5% since the common stock also has price appreciation potential. Bank CDs and money market accounts do not have any such appreciation (or loss) potential. Certain industries, such as utility and energy companies, are known for paying higher dividends than other types of stocks. When interest rates are high and conservative investors are paying 6% to 8% or more, a high-dividend-paying stock may be one that has a dividend in the 5% to 6% range.

Investors who are not in need of current income may be attracted to growth companies: those corporations that pay either no dividend or some nominal amount (i.e., a 1% to 2% dividend). Companies that are able to retain more of their earnings, instead of paying them out to shareholders, have more cash available for growth. Such expansion should lead to greater profitability in the future. The more profitable a corporation is, the more likely the price per share of its stock is going to climb.

Obviously the key is to avoid the losers and load up on the winners. This is certainly easier said than done, despite what market gurus and newsletters may claim. Some well-respected sources say that you should try to buy a stock when it is near its 52-week low; other publications say that you can make money when a stock "breaks out" and starts hitting new highs (presumably this means that the best is yet to come). Neither school of thought can be considered the only rule to follow.

Two Rules

You can do well in the stock market by following two simple rules: (1) diversify and (2) be patient. No matter what someone tells you, no matter how convincing the writer or speaker, no one knows what the stock market will do tomorrow, next month, or next year. Predicting how an individual stock will perform is even more difficult (requiring great doses of luck). We do know that the stock market has always moved in an upward fashion and that the line of advancement is not always straight up. Often, stock prices "stray" and move sideways or even drop. Yet, the market always recovers and goes on to make new highs. Sometimes it takes a week, a year, or five years for that new high to be reached. This is why patience is important. By diversifying and owning shares of several different stocks instead of just one or two, you will decrease your risk significantly.

To show the benefits of being patient and diversifying, consider the following two studies. If you had invested in the stock market for one year at any time during the past half century, your chances of making money would have been over 70%. If, instead, your holding period was extended from one to three or five years, your chances of making money were over 95%. Over any given ten years in a row (1973 to 1982, 1944 to 1953, and so on), the chances of showing a profit were 100%.

Turning to diversification, if you invest in one stock versus a diversified portfolio of ten stocks, your risk level is about five times greater, without any significant increase in return. As you can see, this is an example where risk (lack of diversification) is not commensurate with return (little, if any, return potential is added with a one- or two-stock portfolio).

TAX CONSIDERATIONS

When you own common stocks, there are two potential tax events. First, if the stock pays a dividend, that cash dividend is taxable whether or not it is automatically reinvested, sent directly to you, or invested elsewhere. Dividends are taxable in the year in which they are received. As you may recall, not all corporations pay a dividend.

A few corporations do not pay a cash dividend but instead pay a stock dividend (you get an extra share of stock for every X number of shares you already own). Stock dividends are not taxable until the specific shares (the stock dividend shares) are sold. At the time of sale, the entire net proceeds of the stock dividend shares are fully taxable. For example, if you paid $10 a share for 100 shares of XYZ, received 12 shares of XYZ as a stock dividend, and then later sold the 12 shares for $6 a share, you would show a net taxable capital gain of $72 ($6 times 12 shares). If part or all of the 100 shares were also sold for $6 a share, you would have a capital loss of $4 per share ($10 purchase price minus the $6 selling price).

Capital Gains and Losses

The second tax event that can take place occurs when shares of stock are sold. When you sell stock for less than you paid for it, a capital loss occurs. If, instead, shares are sold for a profit, there is a capital gain. Gains and losses must be reported in the calendar year in which they are sold. Therefore, if you sell stock in February of 2002, your 2002 tax return (which you would file by April 15 of 2003) would show the transaction (a capital gain, loss, or perhaps a break-even situation).

For tax planning purposes, you decide when a stock is to be sold. No one can "force" you to sell a stock, bond, or any other investment for a profit or loss. (The only exception to this rule occurs when a bond or certain kinds of preferred stocks mature.) You may have a large built-in profit on XYZ stock but decide not to sell it this year because you are in a high tax bracket. Instead, you decide to sell it next year when you expect to be in a lower bracket. Similarly, you may own a real dog that has done nothing but go down. You decide to sell it this year (for a capital loss) in order to offset capital gains elsewhere or part of salary.

Controlling Dividends

You cannot control the flow of dividends. If a corporation pays a cash dividend quarterly, you must accept it when it is paid. If you are the owner of the stock, you cannot try to divert a dividend or capital gain to your children or someone else who is in a lower tax bracket. The way to control the amount of dividends you own is either to buy stocks that pay little or no dividends or to own stocks within a qualified retirement plan or variable annuity. Both of these vehicles shelter dividends, interest, and capital gains from current taxation.

ARE STOCKS RIGHT FOR YOU?

Virtually everyone should own common stocks. There are three ways to own common stocks: individually, within a mutual fund, or within a variable annuity. Most people should own common stocks within a mutual fund or within a variable annuity.

Despite the historical record, the majority of people do not have the temperament to own individual stocks. Purchases are often made when the stock is reaching all-time highs, and sales are made at lows (after a stock market crash or correction). In general, people buy stock out of greed and sell out of fear ("the sky is falling," the nightly news people on television say that this is the worst drop in history and things may get worse, and so forth). As a side note, stay away from "hot tips" and "sure things." Some of the worst performing stocks I have ever seen were supposed to do great things—at least that is what the financial gurus or company employees had told me.

Diversify Your Portfolio

If you decide to own individual stocks, make sure your portfolio is diversified. No matter how good your company looks or how hot a particular industry appears, no stock should represent more than 20% of your holdings (5–10% is even better and safer) and that any given industry (auto stocks, computer companies, health care, and so on) does not take up more than 35% of your assets (10% to 20% would be even wiser). These figures may seem too restricting, but consider how your life would change if the stock or industry collapsed. Although such a terrible event may not affect your standard of living now, it could taint your views about owning common stock in the future—and that would be a big, and far-reaching, mistake.

Time Frame and Risk

No one can say with precision that 20% (the national average) or some other percentage of your net worth should be in common stocks or mutual funds that invest in stocks. The weighting should depend upon your risk level and time horizon. If your goals are long term (for example, retire comfortably in 15 to 20 years, send two kids to college in 10 years), then your portfolio should be dominated by stocks (preferably mutual funds so that emotional buy and sell decisions are minimized), even if you are on the conservative side. On the other hand, if your time frame is one or two years, stock ownership, in any form, should be minimal unless you are at least a fairly aggressive investor. The longer your holding period, the more likely it is that you will make money in common stocks.

Portfolio fit and the amount of money that should be earmarked for stocks also depends on the types of stocks you are considering. Some stocks are considered conservative and comparatively safe, such as utility companies; some are considered to be of moderate risk, such as General Motors; other stocks are considered to be somewhat risky, such as Apple Computer; and still others can only be described as a gamble (any start-up company).

As a broad generality, the amount of your portfolio that should be in stocks should range from 20% (retired and conservative) to 90% (middle-aged, working, investing money every year, and at least slightly aggressive). An older individual or couple may not be able to make up a loss in the market, but they also cannot afford not to have some type of hedge against rising prices. Someone in his or her 40s or early 50s who plans on retiring in 15 or more years has time on his or her side. Nevertheless, there are other good investments besides stocks.

If your holding period is about five years or longer, then the bulk of your holdings should be in equities unless you are a conservative investor. If you can live with an investment for 10 or more years, stocks are the preferred choice, even for a conservative portfolio.

Stocks Are the Best Long-Term Investment

As you can see, I strongly favor common stocks. More specifically, I favor mutual funds (see Chapter 6) and variable annuities that own common stocks in their portfolios. Can stocks be scary and uncertain at times? You bet. But so are a lot of other things in life (relationships, job security, health care costs, the price of housing, and so forth). Do people lose money every day in stocks? Yes. But you would lose money in any investment if you panicked. If the loss isn't due to price depreciation, it would be due to purchasing power (buying less with today's dollars than you did yesterday).

Some of you may be thinking that stocks can't be the "best" because you have a friend who made a killing in real estate or art. This is not a fair comparison. If you can choose the piece of real estate or art, then I should be able to pick a specific stock or industry group. I can assure you, if I am allowed such 20-20 hindsight, which is what you would be doing by telling me about a gain after the fact, then there is no chance that any investment can come close to matching common stocks. How many properties or other investments can you show me that have gone up over 1,000% in just a couple of years? Probably none. Yet there are dozens of examples of individual stocks that have done just that.

CHAPTER 5

Utility Stocks

Why utility stocks may be a better choice than corporate bonds
for many conservative investors

UTILITY STOCK BASICS

The traditional view held by brokers and investors alike is that utility stocks are for either old or conservative people. After all, how exciting can it be to own part of a company that produces a pretty boring product and is still largely regulated as to how much it can charge for such a product? All of this may be true, but it certainly has little to do with the actual performance of utility stocks as a whole.

The track record of utilities and utility funds is quite impressive. This is somewhat surprising when you consider that utilities are about as close as you can get to bonds while still being an equity. Part of the reason utilities are sometimes referred to as "bonds in drag" is that the values of these stocks are often highly influenced by interest rates, just as bond values are. The reason for this is twofold: (1) A large part of the attraction of utilities is the comparatively high current dividend they pay out, a dividend that competes, to a degree, with bond yields. (2) Next to paying for fuel or energy transmission, the biggest expense a utilities company incurs is debt service. Utility companies have a lot of outstanding debt that needs to be paid off, interest and principal, on a constant basis.

When interest rates are low, utility companies can sometimes refinance their debt by issuing new, lower-paying bonds. The savings can be tremendous. By paying out less in interest, the utility company has more net profits that can be passed on to its shareholders. The typical utility company pays out more than 80% of its net profits in the form of dividends. Only a modest part is left for expansion, diversification, or other business opportunities. This is not necessarily a bad thing, since investors are attracted to utility stocks because of their dividends and overall stability.

What makes utility stocks different from other investments is that they have little, if any, competition—a unique feature most businesses would like to possess. Imagine not having to worry about a new competitor or a better mousetrap. Granted, certain types of utilities have more competition than others, but that competition is almost always domestic and quite sparse. Furthermore, the demand for utilities is likely to climb each year for the next several decades. Our demand for electricity, water, fuel, and communications seems almost insatiable. As the population increases, so will our demand for these services.

What Are Utility Stocks?

A utility stock represents partial ownership in a utility company, such as a water, telephone, or power plant. As a small owner of the corporation, you participate in the success or shortcomings of the business. If the utility is able to get a rate hike, increase its user base, or add services, shareholders normally benefit in the form of receiving a larger dividend and/or increased value in the stock. Conversely, if the Public Utilities Commission (PUC) continues to deny requests for user costs or the utility company is unsuccessful in one of its ventures (e.g., constructing a nuclear power plant), the price per share of the stock as well as the dividend may be cut.

Normally, the utility company has a monopoly or near monopoly on the service in a particular geographical area. It is this "captive audience" that makes utility stocks so popular. That, and the fact that people are likely to pay their utility bills before their income taxes, makes this investment unlike any other.

There are several ways to participate in utility stocks. If you consider public telephone services to be a growing or stable industry, you can purchase the stock of one or more of the "baby Bells" or buy AT&T. If you are more conservative, buying stock in a water company may be more to your liking. Similarly, if you think electricity and gas bills are too high, you can profit by owning shares of the company that charges such "outrageous rates."

What Are Utility Bonds?

A bond represents part of a corporation's outstanding debt. Owners of this debt do not benefit if the corporation or utility company increases its profitability. Similarly, if a utility company or corporation launches an unsuccessful product or is denied a rate increase, a bondholder will not suffer like a stockholder.

Utility company bonds are rated just like regular corporate bonds. Conceptually, a utility bond should be safer than a corporate bond, since few corporations have a monopoly or near monopoly over their customer base; however, this is not always true. There certainly have been instances where utility companies have branched off into losing ventures or experienced trouble in the area of nuclear power.

A corporation or utility company decides when to issue a bond and how much debt, or additional debt, it is willing to incur. The amount of interest needed to attract buyers of these bonds is pretty much dependent upon the overall bond market (e.g., the general level of interest rates and what other bonds of similar quality and, to a much lesser degree, in a similar industry are paying on their bonds that have the same maturity).

As mentioned in previous chapters, bonds are unique in that a corporation, government, agency, or municipality has made a promise to pay a certain rate of interest and to redeem the instrument when it matures. With stocks, no such promise or guarantee is made, and there is no maturity date.

THE ADVANTAGES OF OWNING UTILITY STOCK

Utility stocks offer several advantages. First, the trading range of most utility companies is fairly predictable; price changes are upward more often than downward. This means that no matter what price you pay per share, there is a good chance that when you go to sell your shares you will see some moderate appreciation. Second, utilities offer some of the very highest dividends when compared with other common stocks. This is because the majority of the profits are paid out to shareholders instead of plowed back into the company for expansion or research purposes. Third, these types of stocks are quite popular. People like owning utility stocks because it is almost like owning a security that is part bond (the high current yield) and part stock (the appreciation potential). In fact, utility stocks, preferred stocks, and convertibles are the closest thing you can get to bonds. Finally, unlike most other industry groups, utilities rarely, if ever, face competition.

Next to the cost of fuel or power, the biggest expense incurred by a utility company is normally the cost of debt. Utility companies typically have a great deal of outstanding debt that must be serviced. The interest paid on these bonds has a major impact on the company's net profits. Furthermore, since utility companies are known for paying a high stock dividend, a great deal of money is sent out quarterly or semiannually to shareholders and bondholders. Thus, the general level of interest rates has a tremendous impact on this industry.

As interest rates fall, utility companies are often able to refinance portions of their total debt at much lower levels. Paying out less in interest makes more money available to shareholders or for corporate reinvestment. Conversely, when interest rates are high, utility profits are squeezed. This type of environment can depress the stock's price and may cause the company to lower its dividend. As mentioned, utility stocks are somewhat like bonds. And, just like bonds, they are quite sensitive to changes in interest rates.

Corporate and utility bonds also offer several advantages. The trading range of good quality bonds is pretty predictable—unless there are swings in interest rates of 1% or more during the year; however, unlike utility stocks, price changes move downward as much or more often than upward. Still, no matter what price you pay per bond, there is a good chance that when you go to sell your bonds, or when they mature, the price you realize will be within 10% of your purchase price. Second, bonds pay a higher current return than utility stocks. This is because the marketplace realizes that there is normally little, if any, appreciation potential with a bond—their chief attraction is yield. Third, bonds remain extremely popular. People like owning bonds because they are easy to understand and there is very little mystery about their future. Finally, the only competition bonds face from conservative investors is other bonds and, to a small degree, utility stocks.

DISADVANTAGES TO OWNING UTILITY STOCK

The disadvantage of utilities is that a provider of electricity may decide to venture into nuclear power (although it has been years since a new plant has been completed or proposed). The construction of these plants has been plagued with delays and huge cost overruns. And, although the long-term monetary consequences of such an addition may be good for the utility company, the short- and medium-term effects can be devastating to both the stock's price and its dividend.

Although utility stocks as a group may have relatively low risk, you need to understand that risks in individual stocks can still be high. Companies with inefficient operation, mismanaged construction projects, hostile regulatory commissions, economically depressed service areas, or botched diversification schemes can and do have problems. Investors should not assume that a monopoly on the local power or gas business assures steady profits. Consider the following:

1. Public Service of New Hampshire filed for bankruptcy in 1988, crushed by cost overruns on a nuclear plant and constant battles with regulators. It was the first utility to do so since the Depression.
2. Of the 97 electric utility companies followed by Value Line Survey (a well-respected stock advisory service), 23—nearly one in four—have reduced or eliminated common stock dividends in the last six years.

3. The major utility companies in California have flirted with bankruptcy throughout 2001.

It is for these reasons that you should focus on mutual funds that specialize in utility stocks, leaving the selection process up to the pros. They are the people who will monitor not only the industry, but the individual companies that comprise the fund's portfolio.

When you buy bonds, you are at the mercy of the marketplace—meaning that if interest rates happen to be low at the time, you will be locking into a similar rate. One to 20 years later, when the bond has matured and it is time to reinvest the principal, the interest rates may be the same or even lower.

When you buy a utility stock or utility mutual fund, there is a strong likelihood that the dividend-income stream will increase over time. This means that you will probably have a good defense against inflation. Moreover, there is also a strong likelihood that you will see appreciation of principal—another way to fight increasing prices. With bonds, there is no such likelihood.

RISK AND RETURN

There are four risks to investing in utilities: the possibility of tremendous rises in fuel costs, a company that branches out into nuclear energy, denial of rate increase requests by the PUC, and interest rate hikes. Unfortunately, there is nothing that can be done to predict whether one or more of these events will occur. However, we have come to learn over the past 20 years that what goes up comes down.

In the early 1980s, energy experts were predicting oil would sell at $50 a barrel. It got down to the $10 range, unadjusted for inflation, by the late 1980s—never coming close to $50. The chances of a utility company constructing a nuclear power plant are much less than they were a decade ago, although brown-outs in California and elsewhere have renewed this discussion. Utility companies are now well aware of public protests, cost escalations, and delays. Requests for rate increases are somewhat political. The PUC is just as likely to permit a rate hike one year and then deny one a few years later. Interest rates work in the same way. Just when it seems that interest rates cannot get any lower (or higher), there is an announcement by the Federal Reserve contradicting what the financial gurus were predicting.

As you might surmise from both of the preceding paragraphs, a patient investor does not really have to worry about any of these "risks." Like other types of stock categories, utilities go up and down, but their long-term trend is always upward.

The biggest risk most bonds and utility stocks face is rising interest rates. When interest rates increase, or there is a fear that they might increase, all bond prices fall—with the possible exception of foreign and high-yield bonds. This is often true with utility stocks, but not always.

BUYING AND SELLING UTILITY STOCKS AND BONDS

Utility stocks can be bought individually or as part of a mutual fund. There are several funds that deal exclusively in utility stocks. If you are attracted to individual issues, but want to make sure that the company you are thinking of going into only deals in hydroelectric power or fossil fuel, you can find out this type of information, and more, by consulting *Value Line*. This stock advisory service describes close to 2,000 different companies, including many utilities. *Value Line* will show you what type of power the company uses, whether nuclear power is anticipated in the future, how successful the provider has been in getting rate increases in the past, and how much outstanding debt there is, as well as future plans, hopes, and concerns.

All utility bonds, like utility stocks, are bought and sold through brokerage firms. The best way to buy and sell bonds is by comparison shopping. Even if you have had a relationship with a specific broker, advisor, or brokerage firm for a number of years, it is worth your time to make a couple of phone calls just prior to making a purchase or sale.

Simply call brokerage firm X and tell them you want to buy (or sell) a specific number of bonds, and then describe the bonds (e.g., the coupon rate, the maturity date, the name of the issuer, and the number of bonds you have or want). Within a couple of minutes, the brokerage firm will give you a specific quote. Once you have this quote, call at least one other firm to see what kind of difference there is in pricing.

After you have finished your comparison, deal with the brokerage firm that gives you the best price. If you are making a sale and your bonds are held at another brokerage firm, phone them immediately and tell them you expect them to match the price at firm X. If they are not willing to match this price, tell them you want them to send you the bond certificate. It will take several weeks for you to get the certificate, but once you have it, you can sell your bonds through any brokerage firm you like.

Unlike utility stocks, which are quoted in the newspaper every day and whose price can later be confirmed for any minute of the trading day, bond pricing is not so readily available. You must make some phone calls, or you will never know how much of a mark-up (hidden commission) you are being charged on the buy or sell side.

Selecting Utility Stocks for Your Portfolio

Utility stocks are an excellent addition to almost any portfolio. High-bracket taxpayers who do not currently own any utility stocks or mutual funds can reposition their retirement accounts or variable annuities to take advantage of this safe and reliable source of income and moderate growth. Low-bracket individuals and couples have more latitude.

Growth-oriented investors often shy away from utility issues, thinking that they do not possess enough appreciation potential. These people are not aware of the power of the dividend compounding year after year. There has been more than one 10- or 15-year period of time when the utility index has outperformed the S & P 500 and the Dow Jones Industrial Average.

Given the choice between utility bonds and utility stocks, both conservative investments, add utility stocks to your portfolio. They have better appreciation potential and, over time, their income stream should be higher. However, bonds are less volatile than even utility stocks, so you might want to include both of these investments as part of your portfolio, particularly if you are a conservative or conservative to moderate investor.

When choosing bond categories, opt for a high-yield corporate or municipal bond fund first and a global or foreign bond fund second. Individual government or agency issues should be your third choice, and high-quality bonds should be your last choice.

TAX CONSIDERATIONS

Unless you are in a low tax bracket, utility stocks are best suited for qualified retirement plans such as IRAs, Keoghs, pension plans, 403(b) plans, 401(k) plans, and profit-sharing plans. Since utilities pay a higher dividend than almost any other industry group, and all such dividends are taxable, only the price appreciation is deferred until a sale.

Even more so than utility stocks, utility bonds are best suited inside some kind of shelter such as a variable annuity or retirement plan. The only way you can get tax relief from bonds outside of such a shelter is to own municipal bonds, also known as "tax-free" bonds.

ARE UTILITY STOCKS RIGHT FOR YOU?

Utility stocks and utility mutual funds are a conservative way to participate in the U.S. stock market. For purposes of added safety, most investors are better off in utility funds, leaving specific security selection, analysis, and ongoing monitoring to full-time professionals. Even an investor who has the vast majority of his or her portfolio in debt instruments (i.e., bonds, CDs, money market accounts, etc.) should have a modest portion in utility stocks. Such an investor would be better served getting rid of some of the debt instruments and buying into this conservative industry group. In fact, the only type of investor who should probably avoid utilities is the very aggressive person who is trying to make a killing (but usually ends up getting "killed" instead).

Utility stocks and utility mutual funds can be an excellent alternative to fixed-income securities for current income and long-term protection from inflation. Some firms have admirable records in this regard: Dallas-based Central & Southwest, for example, has raised its cash dividend every year since 1952.

There are only two categories of bonds I favor: foreign and high-yield. Investors who want bonds as part of their holdings should consider these two categories first; an even better risk-adjusted return could be obtained by including both foreign and high-yield corporate bonds. With both of these categories, it is recommended that you use a mutual fund or variable annuity, since expertise is very important when overseeing either type of bond.

Investors interested in high-quality domestic bonds should buy individual government bonds with a maturity of somewhere between five and 10 years. Such bonds will give you the best risk-reward combination. Individual bonds are recommended for quality domestic issues, because the management and overhead fees associated with mutual funds and even more so with variable annuities eat into the profits too much. More to the point, there is no need for professional management with such safe, easy-to-understand securities.

CHAPTER 6

Mutual Funds

*Why most investors are better off investing in equity (stock)
mutual funds rather than buying individual stocks*

MUTUAL FUND BASICS

As mentioned in the last chapter, when you buy shares of a specific stock, you own individual securities that represent an ownership interest in a corporation. When you buy the company's shares, you are betting on its future and fortunes. If the company increases its profits or earnings, the stock often responds positively. Conversely, if something goes wrong, the price of the corporation's securities may drop.

When you own shares of a mutual fund, you own a very small percentage of a pool of securities (stocks and/or bonds). If you own shares in just one mutual fund, you own part of a portfolio that may be made up of 50 to 100 or more individual securities.

You are no longer betting on how one, two, or even three companies will perform. Instead, you are placing your trust in a portfolio manager who has assembled the stocks of dozens and dozens of companies. The stocks or bonds in the portfolio may represent a specific industry, but are more likely to represent several different segments of the economy.

ADVANTAGES OF MUTUAL FUNDS

Besides being able to substantially eliminate most of the risk of investing in securities (through the diversification inherent in a mutual fund), mutual funds offer many other advantages. Funds provide professional, full-time management. (It's unlikely that you are going to be able to spend eight to 10 hours a day analyzing your portfolio of stocks or bonds.) They also offer you the flexibility of switching from one portfolio to another for a minimal fee. If you owned several different stocks or bonds, the cost of exchanging them for different issues would run into hundreds of dollars, even if you used a discount brokerage firm. With a mutual fund, you can change your investment from, say, a growth fund to a government securities fund by simply making a telephone call.

Systematic Withdrawal Plan

Mutual funds can be structured so that they pay you a monthly income, no matter what types of funds you invest in. With a "systematic withdrawal plan," the fund will send you X dollars (a dollar figure you set) per month. Once your account is set up for a SWP, you never have to request the payment again. Yet, if you want to terminate, suspend, increase, or decrease the service, you can do it at any time, without cost or fee. This one feature offers investors a steady and predictable stream of monthly income, no matter what the stock or bond market is doing. A securities account at a brokerage firm cannot be set up this way.

Good Management

A good mutual fund manager can remove most of the decision-making anxiety that comes with owning an investment that moves up and down in value with the market. This anxiety is what paralyzes many investors—or stops them from participating in "true" investments at all. Do you buy more or sell out when the price drops, or goes up, 10%, 20%, 60%? A disciplined fund manager can look at the situation more objectively and steer a steady course in a troubled market—providing "market rate" returns without a case of shattered nerves.

RISK AND RETURN

When taken as a whole, the track record of mutual funds has been much better than that of individual securities. At first, this may strike you as an odd statement; after all, mutual funds are made up of stocks and/or bonds. But there are plenty of examples of corporations that have gone bankrupt—with their investors losing everything. There is not one example of a mutual fund going out of business with shareholders losing their money.

When you invest in individual securities, there are two types of risk: systematic and unsystematic. Systematic risk refers to that type of risk that cannot be diversified away in the stock or bond market. It represents market risk. Phrased another way, when the stock market takes a beating, a large number of stocks drop in value even though their profits, market share, or quality of management or research has not changed. This type of risk represents 30% of the risk of investing in the stock or bond market.

Unsystematic risk represents the risk that is unique (for better or worse) to a particular corporation. These special features include management style; market share; name recognition; market niche; quality of research and development; or use of a special formula, product, or service. This type of risk represents the other 70% of the "risk pie."

Unsystematic risk can be completely eliminated by diversification (owning shares of just one mutual fund or owning shares of 20 to 30 individual stocks or bonds). Thus, you can eliminate the majority of the risk (70% of the risk pie) associated with stocks or bonds by owning shares of just one diversified mutual fund.

What is surprising about the elimination of unsystematic risk is that it does not substantially decrease your return potential. This is one of the few examples in the world of investing where risk is not commensurate with return. In fact, some studies show that there is no decrease in return potential with a diversified portfolio versus a one-, two-, or three-stock (or bond) portfolio.

As for mutual funds, the biggest risk is chasing last year's winner. The fact that an aggressive growth or bio-tech fund was up 68% last year does not mean that it won't drop by 20% to 50% this year. There is virtually no statistical relationship between a stock, bond, mutual fund, or unit trust's performance from one year to the next. In fact, there is a 50-50 chance that a top-performing fund will be in the bottom half next year, or the year after that.

The other risk you can run if you're investing in mutual funds is in not being properly diversified. Almost all investors are either too conservative (putting most of their money into bond funds, CDs, and money market accounts) or too aggressive (going heavily into specialty or aggressive growth funds). The key to successful investing is to strive for consistently strong returns by building a properly diversified portfolio—as opposed to either being content with slow-moving CDs or, at the other end of the spectrum, trying to double your money in just a couple of years.

BUYING AND SELLING MUTUAL FUNDS

Individual securities and mutual funds are traded in nearly identical ways. Mutual funds offer more options since you can send a check and application directly to the fund company. Many banks and insurance agencies also now provide mutual fund desks where their clients can come in for advice or to make a trade.

If you currently own individual securities and have decided that you'd like to reposition your investments into mutual funds, make sure you take a disciplined approach to the switch. Pick two prices at which you'll sell your individual securities. One should reflect the minimum acceptable gain; the other should reflect the maximum acceptable drop from the current price. When the price of your security reaches either of these points, sell.

You can easily check how your funds are doing. Mutual fund prices are quoted daily in the same sources that list stock prices. All mutual fund owners also receive annual reports from the fund group, which summarize the fund's holdings as of a certain date. Of course, these annual reports are almost always optimistic about the future. It doesn't matter how good or bad last year was, the people writing the report think the future will be terrific.

TAX CONSIDERATIONS

Mutual funds create the same kinds of taxes as individual securities—on current income and on the proceeds from sales. All this income is taxable in the year in which it is received or credited to your account except (1) earnings that have accumulated in a qualified retirement plan; (2) interest and/or dividends in an annuity to the extent that they are not distributed; and (3) interest from tax-free bonds.

Paper profits are not taxable. If you buy an individual security or mutual fund for X and it is now worth (could be sold for) X plus Y, the profit, Y in this example, is a "paper profit" because the asset has not yet been sold. Obviously, if an asset is sold for the same price it was purchased for, there is neither a gain nor a loss. In other words, no taxable event has occurred (somewhat like a paper profit).

Realized Gains and Losses

If you've decided to invest in mutual funds, you should keep in mind that you don't control whether any of the securities in the fund's portfolio will be sold. If your fund decides to sell some of its stocks and/or bonds, the net result will almost certainly be a taxable gain or loss. All the realized gains and losses ("realized" means the security was actually sold) for the calendar year are summed together to determine the net amount of the gain or loss.

At the beginning of the following year, you are sent a Substitute Form 1099, which reports a single dollar figure representing the net capital gain or loss for your investment. This form, sent by the mutual fund group, indicates any dividends and/or taxable interest paid by the fund during the previous calendar year. These items must be reported, meaning that taxes must be paid.

Inheriting Taxable Assests

Upon your death, your beneficiaries inherit your asset(s) based on the fair market value on the date of death. A subsequent sale will result in a taxable gain (to the beneficiary) to the extent that the net sale proceeds exceed the value of the asset on the date of your death. If this figure is less than the fair market value at death, the "new" owner can declare a capital loss (even though the net proceeds may be much higher than the price you paid for the asset). No holding period is required before your beneficiary can sell the investment for a profit or loss. This process applies to mutual funds as well as individual securities, including municipal bonds.

ARE MUTUAL FUNDS RIGHT FOR YOU?

Owning a wide enough range of mutual funds provides the diversification you need. A mutual fund manager can watch over your portfolio full time, with an objectivity and level of attention that most individual investors find impossible. Equally important, the people running these portfolios often have a tremendous amount of experience and access to relevant information that isn't available to the average small investor.

Even if you don't buy any of the standard arguments made in favor of mutual funds (the advantages of professional management, switching privileges, customer service, and so on), the elimination of unsystematic risk that these funds provide should be enough to convince you that mutual funds are the best way to go.

CHAPTER 7

Fixed-Rate Annuities

*Why the guaranteed return, principal protection, and tax benefits of
fixed-rate annuities make this an attractive investment option
for the very conservative investor*

FIXED-RATE ANNUITY BASICS

A fixed-rate annuity is a contractual relationship between the investor and an insurance company, similar to that of the investor and a bank with regard to a CD. For the ability to use your money, the insurance company gives you a set rate of return for a specified period, usually one, three, or five years. At the end of the contract, the investor is free to withdraw part or all of his or her money, transfer it to another annuity issuer, or "roll it over" with the same company, accepting their current rate of return. Money taken out of an annuity prior to its contract expiration date may be subject to a penalty. With most companies, this penalty can't eat into your principal.

Just as with bank CDs, there are a variety of fixed-rate annuities offered by the insurance industry. Some insurance companies offer competitive rates with small penalties that disappear within a few years. Other issuers guarantee only subpar returns and very high "back-end" penalties that go on for a decade or longer.

The rate offered by annuities goes along somewhat with the prime interest rate. As you might imagine, contract rates have also varied quite a bit over the past several decades. Since interest rates steadily dropped throughout most of the 1980s and early 1990s, this means that initial and renewal rates offered by annuities also dropped by several percentage points.

For the most part, in the past, annuity rates have been higher than those offered by bank CDs. There is no indication that this trend will soon change.

Money invested in an annuity grows and compounds tax-deferred, making it a somewhat unique investment vehicle. Fixed-rate annuities are also one of the few investments in which the principal is guaranteed each and every day.

When you buy a fixed-rate annuity, your rate of return is locked in for the guarantee period. This rate remains level during this period, whether you take out some of your money or liquidate the entire contract.

Fixed-rate annuities have been an extremely popular investment for several decades now because they are easy to understand, they feature the very popular "guarantee" of future earnings, and they are sometimes one of the few options available to participants in a qualified retirement plan. If you want an investment that will let you know exactly what rate of return you will get and how long that rate will remain in effect, and you want to make sure that your principal remains intact and that it can be gotten to at any time, then an annuity is something you should look into.

An Example

For example, suppose you have $10,000 you want to invest somewhere safe. You look at bank CDs but are unimpressed by the interest rate they are offering and do not want to incur a penalty in an emergency situation that could eat into part of your original investment. You also look at money market accounts and U.S. Treasury bills but do not want the interest rate to fluctuate during the next couple of years.

You discover that annuities are paying 1% or 2% more than bank CDs or other similarly conservative investments. The annuity is paying 7% for five years. (This means that your account will be worth $10,700 [$10,000 times 1.07] in one year, $11,449 in two years, $12,250 in three years, $13,108 in four years, and $14,026 in five years, when the guarantee ends.) At the end of the con-tracted-for period, the insurance company sends you a letter telling you that the new rate for the next year will be, for this example, 8%. If you do not notify them within the next 30 days, the entire account will be rolled over automatically and your investment, principal plus all the interest accumulated during the previous five years, will begin earning 8%. However, you discover that 8% is not as high as you can get from another annuity company or from your local bank or bro-kerage firm. You simply contact the company that holds your money and tell them to either send you a check or transfer the money to a different insurance company. That is all there is to it.

If it turns out that the company you are using continues to offer a rate you feel good about, you never have to do anything. At the end of each guarantee period, which may be anywhere from one to 10 years, the annuity issuer will send you a letter informing you as to the new rate for the next period and pointing out that if you do nothing the investment will continue.

Withdrawals

While you own an annuity, you are free to make withdrawals. You do not have to give a reason as to why part or all of the interest or principal is needed. Withdrawal requests must be in writing. By law, most companies must send you a check within seven days. Often, a check can be sent out or wired even faster. Some companies let you make withdrawals several times a year; others restrict this privilege to one request per annum.

However, it is not always this easy and painless. Some companies charge a penalty for withdrawal for a couple of years after the guarantee period ends. This means that refusal to renew the contract for the next couple of years at, for example, 6% could mean that you have to pay a penalty to get at your money; there is even a chance that the IRS will level its own separate penalty.

More on Penalties

Speaking of penalties, when your advisor checks out different contracts for you, make sure he or she tells you the penalty schedule. In particular, you want to know about the free withdrawal privilege, the bailout provision, and the penalty percentage that could be imposed and its duration.

The free withdrawal privilege refers to how much you can take out each year without cost or penalty. Most annuities allow you to take out up to 10% each year for free. If you buy a one-year "CD/annuity," your entire account can be liquidated at the end of the year without cost. Otherwise, most companies charge about a 5% penalty for excess withdrawals. What this means is that if you have a $10,000 annuity that grows to $11,000, you can take out $1,000 without penalty; amounts in excess of $1,000 are penalized 5%. Thus, for example, if the contract owner needed $1,500, he or she could take out $1,000 for free and then pay a $25 penalty for the remaining $500 (5% of $500).

The bailout provision is a clause designed to protect you against the insurance company's offering you a low renewal rate. Suppose you invest in an annuity that has a 5% penalty for the first five years and a guaranteed rate of 8% for the first three years, with a "7% bailout." At the end of three years, the insurance company notifies you that the renewal rate for years four through six will be 6.9%. Since 6.9% is less than 7%, this means that you can withdraw all of your money, or transfer it to another insurer without cost, fee, or penalty. This penalty-free election was due to the fact that when you first went into the investment, the insurance company basically said, "Look, we are going to give you

8% for three years. At the end of three years, if we don't give you at least 7%, you can get out, without cost, and without giving us a reason." However, with a 7% or higher renewal rate, you would either have to accept the new rate or be subject to whatever penalty was remaining (5% in this example).

The penalty period for annuities ranges anywhere from zero to 10%. The most common penalty, 5%, either declines by 1% each year for five years or remains level (5% penalty if excess withdrawals are made during any of the first five years). As for penalty schedules, there is quite a variety. Even though close to 80% of all those who invest in annuities never make withdrawals, this is still something that should be checked out. Nevertheless, out of fairness to the annuity industry, it should also be pointed out that if an emergency does arise, presumably the investor has other sources of capital that can be tapped without cost or penalty.

ADVANTAGES OF FIXED-RATE ANNUITIES

There are three reasons why people buy fixed-rate annuities: (1) safety of principal and interest, (2) a specific rate of return, and (3) no initial or ongoing fees or commissions.

The most unique feature of fixed-rate annuities is that they have been around in this country for over 100 years and few investors have ever lost principal. This almost perfect track record is only matched or exceeded by certain insurance products and securities backed or guaranteed by the U.S. government. However, unlike government obligations, one's principal (initial investment plus any ongoing contributions) is guaranteed every day; when you own a government bill, note, or bond, face value is only guaranteed if the investment is held until maturity. You could invest $250,000 in a fixed-rate annuity and know that tomorrow, next week, or next month you could call the whole thing off and get back a check for at least $250,000, no matter what the insurance company penalty might be.

Safety of principal is the reason why tens of billions of dollars are invested in annuities each year. When you go into a fixed-rate annuity, there are no surprises. The insurance company or broker tells you exactly how much money you are going to earn. Unlike other investments, the rate of return doesn't change weekly or monthly. To calculate how much money you are going to earn, simply multiply your principal (the amount of money you are going to invest) by the quoted interest rate. The resulting figure represents how much your account will grow during the first year.

If the annuity has a guaranteed rate for two or more years, take your principal plus the interest earned from the first year, add the two figures together, and then multiply this combined number by the stated rate of return. This will show you how much the account will earn for year two; the process can be repeated for as many years as the guarantee lasts. If the company tells you that the guarantee period is seven years, you will get the rate they have promised you, compounded, for each of the next seven years, no matter what the stock market does, how far up or down the prime interest rate goes, or how profitable the insurance company is.

When you buy an annuity, you don't pay any commissions or fees; 100% of your money goes to work for you immediately. Nothing is taken out for a broker or paid to the insurance company. The advisor or person who sells you the annuity may receive a commission from the insurance company, but any such dollar benefit is paid by the insurance company—it doesn't come out of the client's pocket.

DISADVANTAGES OF FIXES-RATE ANNUITIES

As you might have guessed, no investment is this good without having some strings attached to it. There are four disadvantages to fixed-rate annuities: (1) the rate offered may not be competitive; (2) there is a fluke chance that your principal, and any accumulated growth or interest, could be tied up for a few years if the issuer becomes troubled; (3) money taken out early may be subject to penalty; (4) there is no guarantee that the renewal rate will be competitive.

Hundreds of companies offer annuities. Some issuers offer high rates of return; others have low rates. Companies that advertise less than competitive rates are not necessarily any more financially secure or better than companies that have high rates. Often, the salesperson or advisor who is trying to put you into a low-yielding annuity has either not done any comparison shopping, is a "captive" broker and limited to the number or types of annuities he or she can offer, or is receiving special compensation (a higher fee or commission).

Although extremely remote, there is always a chance that the insurance company that is backing your fixed-rate annuity will run into financial difficulty in the future. For this reason, if you have a large sum of money, say $50,000 or more, you should split it up and invest in two or more fixed-rate annuities. The other way to counter this disadvantage, as well as the one described in the preceding paragraph, is to make sure your advisors do their homework. Have them review annuities offered by several companies, studying the rating(s) as well as the rate of return being offered.

If the Issuer Fails

The problem of financial insolvency of companies that issue annuities has been greatly exaggerated. Nevertheless, to be on the safe side, you should limit your exposure to any one insurance company, just as you would if you had over $100,000 to invest in a bank. Only a few states do not have a guaranty fund (fees are charged annually by the state's insurance commissioner and used to protect policyholders). Every state that does have such a safety net limits its liability; in the case of annuities, protection is normally limited to $100,000.

When a company does run into money problems and the state is forced to suspend its operations, what usually happens is that the issuer is required to take certain steps. If these measures are not successful or the losses are just too severe, other insurance companies will usually step in. The competition hopes to be able to take over the faulting company's assets and all its contract owners. Thus, a state's guaranty fund is rarely used; the private sector comes to the rescue. Of course, the successful bidder doesn't bail out a troubled peer simply out of the kindness of its heart. In return for preserving their account, contract owners must accept the victor's terms. Typically, this means that investors' monies are tied up for three to five years and the interest rate during this period may not be as high as the then going rate. Withdrawals during this "reorganization period" are subject to sometimes severe penalties.

Additional Caveats

One of the arguments used in favor of fixed-rate annuities is that there is no chance for loss of principal. This is true, except in the case of a "market-rate adjusted" annuity wherein there could be some loss or gain of principal—similar to owning a bond. But, this "guarantee of principal at all times," which is found with traditional fixed-rate annuities, is oversold, because there are plenty of highly rated municipal bonds that have maturities ranging from less than a year to up to 30 years and everything in between. By opting for a specific maturity that coincides with your financial plan, there is no chance of a loss as long as the bond is held to maturity and it is not purchased for a premium (meaning a price above its redemption or maturity value). The one exception to this statement would be if you bought a bond that defaulted—something that is rare with municipal bonds and extremely rare with highly rated bonds.

Another reason for the popularity of fixed-rate annuities, not often mentioned, is that bankers, brokers, and financial planners like to sell them, because they are an easy sale and include a commission to the selling broker of approximately 4%. The commission is not paid directly by the client. Note the words not paid directly: the investor is paying the commission by accepting potential penalties and a rate of return that is lower than what he or she could reasonably get elsewhere.

RISK AND RETURN

Fixed-rate annuities face the same risk that most of the investments shown in this book possess: purchasing power risk (inflation). Fortunately, their historic rates of return, coupled with faster growth due to tax-deferral (an important feature outside a qualified retirement account), means that this investment has a much better chance of outpacing inflation than most of the more traditional, safe investments.

A second risk is the chance of losing part of the accumulated account value due to an insurance company penalty. This penalty can eat into part, and occasionally all, of the interest gained in the account, but it cannot cut into the investor's principal. Any penalty risk can be completely eliminated by making sure that withdrawals are equal to or less than the free withdrawal privilege provided by the insurer.

The final risk, a non-competitive renewal rate, can be avoided ar minimized in a couple of ways. First, make sure any penalty period coincides with the guaranteed rate period. Thus, if the rate guarantee is, say, 6% for five years, the penalty period should be five years or less. If the penalty period is longer than the initial guaranteed rate period, deal with a company whose policy is to credit the renewals at the same level as new money. This gives you the assurance that the insurance company will stay competitive in the future (otherwise they would have trouble attracting new clients). Finally, consider only investing in annuities that have a relatively short penalty period (zero to three years) so that when the contract matures, the annuity can be moved tax-free to another company (what is known as a "1035 exchange") or rolled over with the same company, provided they have a competitive rate.

BUYING ANNUITIES

Even though all annuities are offered only by insurance companies, this investment instrument is sold and marketed through banks, brokerage firms, and financial planners. Since there is no cost or fee involved, your decision as to what person or firm to choose should be based on variety (the number of companies/policies they represent), competence (the advisor's knowledgeability), and integrity (the person's honesty and willingness to tell you all of a contract's advantages and disadvantages).

You can purchase an annuity directly from an insurance company, but there is no advantage to doing this; in fact, it may be a disadvantage. What I mean by this is that the company knows nothing about you. They cannot guide you as to whether you should favor, for example, a one-, two-, or three-year locked-in rate (contract); and they won't tell you about what the competition is offering.

You can make the investment by filling out a one-page application and writing a check directly to the insurance company. You begin earning interest as soon as the insurer has received the application and check. The contract, which also doubles as your confirmation, is sent out about three weeks later. Annuity contracts are more extensive than mutual fund or stock confirmations, which is why it takes so long to get the initial acknowledgment.

By law, every annuity contract includes a "seven-day free-look" provision. Once you receive your contract in the mail, you have up to seven days to return it to the insurance company and get a full refund. Investors rarely do this, but it is nice to know that you have a chance to review the contract before making a final commitment. Some states have a thirty-day free-look period, meaning you have up to thirty days to get all of your money back.

Statements are sent out once a year. If a contract owner wants to know the value of his or her account during the year, a phone call can be made to the insurance company. There is really no need to check a contract's value prior to receiving the annual statement, since you can't lose money in an annuity—it literally goes up in value each day.

TAX CONSIDERATIONS

A chief reason people buy annuities is for their tax benefits. The benefits come in two forms: during accumulation and during withdrawal. When you invest in an annuity, your money grows and compounds indefinitely. In fact, you don't have to make a single withdrawal while you and/or your spouse are alive. Unlike a qualified retirement plan, such as an IRA, Keogh, or profit-sharing plan, there is no age limit as to when you must start taking money out.

Between 70% and 85% of all investors who buy annuities end up never taking money out of them. For most people, then, the question becomes: What happens when a spouse, children, or other beneficiaries inherit the account? If your spouse inherits the account, he or she is not required to make any withdrawals. If the beneficiary is someone other than your spouse, the IRS does not require the account to be liquidated by the beneficiary(s) for up to five years. During this five-year period, the new owner also does not have to make any withdrawals. He or she is free to wait until the last day of the fifth year to close out the account. Remember, spouses are not under any type of deadline.

Money withdrawn by an heir, spouse, child, friend, and so forth, is not subject to any IRS or insurance company penalty. Death of the annuitant is not considered a "voluntary" event, therefore any remaining penalties are waived.

Taxes on Withdrawals

Withdrawals of income and/or growth are fully taxable; distributions of principal are never taxed. Unfortunately, you do not have a say in what part of the annuity is being liquidated. You can't go to the IRS or to the insurance company and ask them to distribute your principal first (unless you have an annuity you purchased before 1981). Whether you call it accumulated growth or income, this is what comes out first. For example, if a $25,000 initial investment grew to $40,000, the first $15,000 would be fully taxable. It would make no difference whether the entire $15,000 came out at once or $1,000 came out this year, $700 the following year, and so on. Once all of the account was depleted except for the original $25,000, the taxation would cease and the final $25,000, in this example, would be considered a return of principal and therefore not subject to any state or federal income taxes.

On the positive side, only the withdrawals are subject to income tax (and a 10% IRS penalty if money is taken out before age 59½, death, or disability). Money that remains in the account is not subject to a penalty or tax and continues to grow tax-deferred. There is only one way to avoid taxation of all of the initially withdrawn money: annuitization.

Annuitization

Annuities are the only investment in the world that can be structured to provide you or someone else with income for life. You may do this by opting for lifetime annuitization (which could be over the life of you and/or your spouse, child, parent, friend, and so on). By making such a choice, the investor receives monthly income until he or she dies. In the case of a couple, married or otherwise, the contract can be set up so that payments remain level until the second partner or friend dies.

Annuitization is something you must request. When you annuitize, you are telling the insurer (and the IRS) that you want to liquidate the entire contract over at least a five-year period. The period you choose can be longer than five years, but it can't be shorter if you want to receive some tax benefits. Upon receiving a request for annuitization, the insurance company makes a computation and determines your exclusion ratio. The exclusion ratio shows how much of each distribution is considered to be a return of principal (not taxable) and how much is growth and/or income (fully taxable). Thus, if your agent tells you that your exclusion ratio is going to be, say, 85%, then only 15% of each check you receive will be taxable. These potentially tremendous tax benefits continue until 100% of the investor's principal has been received. Depending on how long the owner has opted to annuitize, this could take anywhere from five years to a lifetime. The longer the annuitization period, the smaller the exclusion ratio.

There are two potential disadvantages to annuitization: (1) having the payout schedule locked in and (2) having a future accumulation rate that is usually less than a competitive rate. Let's look at each of these points separately. First, once you begin annuitization with all but a few companies, you can't stop the process. Therefore, if you opt for a lifetime payout schedule (monthly payments lasting until one or more people die—for example, lasting until both the husband and wife are deceased), you could not later change your mind. It makes no difference if there is a death, bankruptcy filed, or an unforeseen emergency; the timing and the amount of the payments will not change in any way. Second, once annuitization is selected, the growth rate on the account balance that hasn't yet been distributed will not continue to grow at a fair rate. If your insurer was paying you 6%, this rate will probably stop once annuitization begins, and the rate from that point forward will most likely be in the 3% to 4% range. This is not always the case, but it is more the rule than the exception. A few companies offer a very competitive yield during annuitization. If your insurer doesn't offer a competitive rate, keep in mind the following points: (1) The rate you have received up to this point (the value of the account) will not be affected. (2) You do not have to annuitize with your current contract carrier; the contract can be exchanged tax-free with another insurance company.

Investors are never required to annuitize. It should only be chosen if (1) tax-advantaged income is needed now, (2) the company selected is quoting a fair and competitive rate, and (3) it is understood that once the process begins, it cannot be stopped, altered, or amended.

ARE FIXED-RATE ANNUITIES RIGHT FOR YOU?

Fixed-rate annuities are for the very conservative; there are few things in this world as safe and secure. It is the historical and financial safety of the insurance industry that makes fixed-rate annuities such a safe bet. The ability of an investor to choose among guaranteed rates of return for anywhere from a single quarter up to 10 years makes this a flexible and appealing investment. Moreover, this is the only investment that allows you to lock in a rate of return for life (by annuitizing).

Annuities are a clear choice for the investor who is looking for the utmost in safety, wants a competitive or better than average return (yield), and has the understanding that because of the insurance company penalty, annuities are not an alternative to highly liquid investments such as money market accounts, T-bills, and CDs that mature in just a few months.

Over $100 billion was invested in annuities last year. This is a very popular investment that is still not understood by the majority of investors or brokers.

I discuss annuities in depth in my books, *All About Annuities* and *The 100 Best Annuities You Can Buy*. If you read either of these books, you will learn that I actually like annuities; but I like variable annuities (similar features to a fixed-rate annuity but the investor's return or loss depends on the performance of the selected subaccounts—similar to a mutual fund family) and only favor fixed-rate annuities for the conservative investor or the misinformed investor whose only alternative would be something like a bank CD.

CHAPTER 8

Bonds

*Why the safety, tax-free interest, price stability, flexibility,
and marketability of municipal bonds make them
a viable option for longer-term investing*

BOND BASICS

All bonds are debt instruments. Bonds are issued by corporations, governments, and municipalities as a way of raising money without allowing the investor a means of participating in the future growth of the entity. Corporations, governments, and municipalities also issue notes, which are simply debt instruments with a shorter maturity—usually one year or less in the case of municipalities and corporations. Such notes are common instruments inside money market funds.

A bond is like an IOU. The issuer of the bond issues a debt instrument that has a specific maturity and pays a specific rate of interest. The amount of interest paid depends upon (1) the quality of the issuer, (2) the bond's maturity, and (3) current interest rates. The entity issuing the bond promises to pay the investor the face value of the bond when it matures. For the privilege of borrowing your money, the entity also agrees to pay you interest twice a year until the bond matures or is "called away" (redeemed prematurely). The redemption value may be slightly higher if the bond is called away before its natural maturity date by the issuing corporation or municipality. Government bonds cannot be called away; they have no "call feature."

When the bond matures, the issuer pays you the face amount of the bond. The face amount paid may be more or less than what you paid for the security. If you end up receiving less than what you paid for the bond, this means that you originally paid a premium for it (you paid more than face value). If the value at maturity is more than what you paid for the bond, you got it at a discount (you paid less than face value). As odd as it might sound, discounts and/or premiums are not necessarily good or bad. Determining if a purchase price was, in hindsight, a good or bad deal depends upon how much interest you received and how much you got at the end, when the bond came due. In other words, you need to look at the "whole enchilada"—the total return.

What is somewhat unique about bonds is that if they are held to maturity, the investor is pretty much assured that he or she will receive the face value of the bond; there is no such maturity date or assurance with common stocks. If the bond is not highly rated, the company may enjoy a turnaround, thus improving its rating and causing the bond to increase in value by several percentage points. Bonds are also special since most of them pay interest semiannually (GNMAs and FNMAs pay interest and some principal monthly). Most other interest-bearing instruments pay interest daily, weekly, or monthly.

Municipal Bonds

Municipal bonds have been in existence since 1895, when the U.S. Supreme Court recognized reciprocal immunity (meaning the states can't tax the feds and the feds can't tax the states). Municipal bonds are issued by states, counties, and municipalities as a means of financing public works such as street lights, libraries, roads, and airports. The municipality issues you a bond, which represents their promise to pay the face amount of the bond when it matures along with interest payments every six months. Besides levying taxes, charging fees, and receiving funds from the federal government, this is the only way a municipality is able to raise money. One could say that municipalities are just like the U.S. government: They spend more than they take in and therefore have to issue bonds in order to help pay for some of these "excesses" (almost all states have a constitution that requires them to have a balanced budget).

Since you can't buy stock in a county or state, municipalities must issue bonds or notes (notes are like short-term bonds) if they wants to raise money other than through taxes and fees. Municipal bonds share many of the same characteristics of government and corporate bonds, but there are differences, mostly in their advantages.

High-Yield (Junk) Bonds

One of the most overlooked areas of bonds is the high-yield sector, also known as the junk bond sector. When most investors think of junk or high-yield bonds, the first thing that comes to mind is high risk. Although this can certainly be the case when you are talking about corporate bonds that have low ratings, the same thing cannot really be said about municipal that are either rated below investment grade or simply NR (not rated).

High-yield tax-free issues, like their corporate peers, have different ratings; and just like junk corporate bonds, there are certainly categories that should be avoided. Nevertheless, if you stick to the top two or three grades of junk, you should be amply rewarded for the additional risk. High-yield municipal have a current yield that is about one and a half points higher than an A, AA, or AAA municipal issue. This enhanced yield, which can be an increase in return of over 25% (4% times 1.25 equals 5%, which is what high-yield tax-frees were yielding at the time this book was written), also provides a second advantage to the investor: less volatility during normal economic conditions. The higher the yield of a bond, the less it will fluctuate when interest rates go up or down.

The percentage of defaults the junk sector of tax-frees has seen is very small, much smaller than what high-yield corporate bonds have experienced. What makes high-yield tax-frees somewhat of a hidden treasure is that they have been painted with the same brush that has tainted certain corporate bonds. It is for this reason that investors who are in a moderate or high tax bracket should consider diversifying their tax-free portfolios with some bonds that offer a higher yield. Owing to the increased financial risk, it is recommended that these bonds be purchased within a unit trust (which is a fixed portfolio of books) or fund in which there are experts to constantly evaluate the economic environment and the financial well-being of the issuers.

ADVANTAGES TO OWNING BONDS

There are three advantages to owning bonds: (1) safety, (2) flexibility, and (3) marketability. And for municipal bonds there are two more: tax-free interest and comparative price stability.

Bonds are an extremely safe investment. Other than obligations guaranteed or backed by the U.S. government and certain insurance policies and fixed-rate annuities, nothing is safer than municipal bonds. The default rate of municipal bonds has been extremely small since their introduction more than a century ago.

Flexibility is a feature common to all bonds. You can buy a bond that matures in the number of years you choose. For example, if you want to invest for an event that will take place 14 years down the road (for example, to buy a retirement home, to buy a vehicle, to pay for a vacation, or to pay tuition bills), and you want the face value of the bonds you buy to be available, you can find bonds that mature in 14 years. In terms of marketability, if you ever want to sell your bonds before their maturity date, there is a large marketplace ready to buy them from you at a fair price. It takes less than five minutes to buy or sell a municipal bond, whether you are dealing with $5,000 or $5 million worth of bonds.

Like other bonds, municipal securities pay interest twice a year; unlike other bonds, this interest is tax-free. There is also the benefit of relative price stability. When interest rates go up and down, so do the value of bonds. Municipal bonds, however, are less volatile, or susceptible, to interest-rate movements than corporate or U.S. government bonds that have a similar maturity. The tax-free interest is the most unique feature of municipal bonds. When all is said and done, it is the real return of this investment that makes it different from other debt instruments. Once you subtract the effects of taxes and inflation from most bond investments, the return is often negative or only slightly positive. When you own municipal bonds, the real return is often positive by two or three percentage points.

DISADVANTAGES OF BONDS

There are only two possible disadvantages with bonds: (1) price fluctuation and (2) potential for default. As mentioned, bonds go up and down in value. This doesn't mean that your interest rate or yield varies—it remains the same. In fact, if you don't plan on selling your bonds before they mature, then you probably shouldn't be concerned with changing values. However, if an emergency arises or you see a better investment opportunity, keep in mind that your purchase price may be higher or lower than your selling price.

When interest rates increase, bond values fall; when rates fall, bond values (your principal, not your interest payment) increase. The amount of price variance depends upon how much rates increase and the remaining maturity of the bond. The greater the change in rates and length of time before maturity, the greater the price movement, for better or for worse. However, municipal bonds experience only one-third to one-half the fluctuations that similar corporate or government bonds experience. It may seem strange that municipal move up and down less than governments, but the reason for this is quite logical: demand versus supply. The high demand for tax-free bonds, compared with the outstanding supply, causes prices to change only modestly during any given year.

The second issue is that of default. As with all other investments, other than those backed by or insured by the U.S. government or one of its agencies (i.e., GNMA, FNMA, etc.), there is always a chance that your bond issuer may become a victim of troubled times. This risk can be avoided or minimized in one of two ways. First, you can buy municipal bonds that are insured, as to both the semiannual interest payments and the face value at maturity. Insured municipal bonds are quite common. Second, you can limit your purchases to bonds that are highly rated (AAA, AA, A, or BAA). If your comfort level necessitates you owning only AA rated bonds and your issue has a rating change from AA to A, you can quickly sell the bond and buy a new security that is AA or AAA rated.

The issue of default is often blown out of proportion. Only a small fraction of 1% of all quality municipal bonds have ever become troubled. Even then, this does not spell complete disaster. Studies indicate that defaulting bonds usually means that the investors lose about 25% of their principal, on average. No loss is "good," but at least these figures should make you feel quite a bit better.

RISK AND RETURN

As a broad generality, bonds usually have about half the volatility of common stocks. Depending upon quality, maturity, and financial conditions, some bonds exhibit even greater price movement while others have virtually no volatility. This makes their day-to-day value more stable, a benefit to an investor who may have to raise money at an unexpected time. Bonds also accrue interest every day. This means that if you sell a bond a month before it is about to make its semi-annual interest payment, you receive market value for the bond plus five months worth of interest. Someone who sells a stock before it pays its quarterly dividend (assuming the stock pays a dividend) is not entitled to any part of the dividend.

Corporate bonds are considered a "senior obligation," meaning that if the company falls on hard times, it must pay the owners of all its bonds the interest they are entitled to before making any payment to stockholders. A corporation's board of directors can decide to eliminate or lower its stock dividend at any time. They do not have such powers over their bonds. Failure to pay bondholders 100% of their semiannual interest payment could result in a lawsuit in which a judge determines that the corporation must take a specific course of action to fulfill its solemn promise to its bondholders.

Bondholders do not participate in the success of the issuer. This means that the only upside potential a bond could experience is when interest rates are going down or are expected to go down. Conversely, a bondholder can see his or her interest drop in value if rates go up or there is a fear that rates are going to increase.

The track record for bonds has been mediocre compared to common stocks. Of course, the difference in performance figures doesn't tell the whole story. First, the bond investor will have most likely experienced much less upward and downward volatility than the stock investor. Second, there have certainly been extended periods when bonds have outperformed stocks (e.g., a huge number of stocks dropped more than 50% during 2000 and the first part of 2001, yet bond values increased during that same period), and such periods are sure to occur in the future. Still, once you factor in the effects of inflation and income taxes (which would not apply to the interest payments from municipal bonds), bonds have experienced real gains of only about 1% to 2% a year over the past half century.

Three Risks

Three risks are associated with domestic bonds: (1) purchasing power risk, (2) interest-rate risk, and (3) default risk. With government and agency issues, there is no default risk. Furthermore, the default rate on high-quality bonds is extremely low. This means that the risk of default is pretty much a nonissue except with bonds that have poor ratings (for example, CCC, CC, C, and D).

All bonds have interest-rate risk (meaning when interest rates change or there is a belief that they might change, the value of the underlying bonds can go up or down). Interest-rate risk can be greatly reduced by owning bonds that have a maturity of five years or less. Bonds with a remaining maturity of 10 years have approximately half the interest-rate risk as those with remaining maturities of 20 to 30 years. That leaves purchasing power risk.

There is no way to avoid purchasing power risk (the cumulative effects of inflation). For example, when you buy $20,000 worth of 10-year bonds, the bonds will mature in 10 years and you will get your $20,000 back, but its purchasing power will have decreased somewhere between 25% and 65%. The interest payments along the way can be reinvested in other bonds or securities to offset such a loss, but such reinvestment may not be enough, particularly if the interest payments are fully taxable.

Fluctuating Yields

Yields on tax-free issues have moved up and down in a fashion similar to other government or corporate bonds. The decade of the 1980s was an extremely good period for municipal bonds. The combination of high current yields and falling interest rates (appreciation of principal) provided minus with total returns that had never been seen before. Although principal remains stable, you should know that the income stream from a tax-free bond *fund* or *unit trust* will fluctuate, sometimes for the better, sometimes for the worse. The variations are due to a changing portfolio. In the case of a bond fund, new issues are being added all the time as investors add or redeem shares. When new money added to a fund or a bond in the fund's portfolio is redeemed or is "called away," it is replaced by another bond. This new bond may have a yield that is a little higher or lower than what it is replacing. The "replacements" are added to the existing portfolio, slightly altering the current yield. As interest rates move upward, so do returns in a bond fund. When rates drop, so do yields on muni funds.

A unit trust, also referred to as a unit investment trust (UIT), is different from a fund. A unit trust is a fixed portfolio of bonds. The yield on unit trusts changes when a bond is either called away or redeemed. In the case of a unit trust, the bond is not replaced. Proceeds from the bonds that are no longer in the portfolio are distributed to the unit holders (you and everyone else who owns this particular unit trust). As you might suspect, when a bond, or series of bonds, is removed from the trust, the yield goes down. This is because bonds are not called away by the issuer unless the municipality can issue a new security at a lower rate. This fact does not make unit trusts better or worse than individual bonds or funds; it just makes them different.

For practical purposes, if you choose a good quality muni, unit trust, or fund, your only real risk is potential loss of purchasing power. It may sound wonderful to hear 5%, 6%, or 7% tax-free, but if inflation is 8%, 9%, or 10%, you are losing purchasing power. Often it is difficult even to imagine that inflation will ever reach these levels in the United States. But as unlikely as this situation is, it is something that you should at least be conscious of.

BUYING AND SELLING BONDS

You buy and sell bonds (municipal, corporate, or government) by seeing or telephoning your broker. Tax-free bonds are sold by brokerage firms, financial planners and advisors, municipal bond specialty houses, and even banks and savings and loan associations. Your counselor can show you a wide range of maturities (ranging anywhere from less than a year to 30 years), yields (different returns on your investment), quality (from AAA all the way down to different grades of "junk bonds"), and prices (face value, also referred to as par, premiums, and discounts).

The type, quality, maturity, price, and yield that is best for you can be determined by your financial expert. You may find that you know exactly what you want and don't need any outside counseling. One of the nice features of municipal bonds is that you don't pay a commission when you buy or sell them. The brokerage firm you deal with, whether it's a discount or full-service firm, will mark up the bonds (this is how they are compensated), but such a fee can be less than one-fourth of a point (less than a fourth of a percent). This fee, or charge, is very reasonable and will probably have very little, if any, effect on your return.

Bonds in Bunches

You can also own municipal bonds indirectly by buying a "packaged product" such as a municipal bond fund or unit trust. A bond fund allows you to move your money around within the fund family. Thus, if you later decide that minus are not for you, you can switch, for only $5, from the XYZ Tax-Free Fund into the XYZ Growth Fund.

If you wish to get out of a unit investment trust, you can do so without cost or fee; but your money would then have to be invested with another company or product. This restriction is not a big concern, but it may be important to those investors who like the convenience of being able to move easily from one investment into another.

Bond Prices

Bond prices are most frequently quoted in $^{1}/_{8}$ points on a scale of 1 to 100; each point represents $10, and a half point represents $5. Since bonds have a face value of $1,000 each, a price of 100 equals 100% of $1,000; a price of 98 equals 98% of $1,000 (or $980 per bond). A bond that sells for exactly $1,000 is selling for "par" (or face value). Any price below 100 ($1,000) is considered to be a discount, and any price above 100 means that the bond is selling for a premium (some price over $1,000 per bond). Thus, a bond selling for 101 and ¼ is selling for $1,010 (101% of $1,000) plus $2.50 (¼ of a point). A bond selling for 98 and ½ is selling for $985 ($980 plus ½ of $10).

When you own an individual bond, the bond issuer (for example, the XYZ Corporation or the ABC Municipality) may be able to call away your security (force you to sell it back to them at a specified price). Bonds in a mutual fund are not immune from such events, but if you're participating in this market through a fund, you don't have to do anything about it—the fund manager will receive the prepayment and invest the money in other bonds.

Fees

There is a fee whenever you buy or sell a bond. This fee is really a commission, but it doesn't show on your confirmation or monthly statement; it's rarely even mentioned by the broker handling the transaction. These fees are instead called mark-ups, and can range anywhere from a small fraction of 1% ($10 per bond) all the way up to 5% ($50 per bond). The amount you pay depends upon your broker, the yield of the bond, and its maturity. A similar mark-up is charged when you sell a bond prior to its natural maturity. This means that if your broker is selling some of your bonds and says, "I can get you 99 each," you will receive $990 per bond. The broker doesn't tell you how much the brokerage firm is making on the transaction (although you can always request such information).

Knowing the Value

The value of a unit trust or fund can be quickly determined by telephoning the company's toll-free number. During business hours on any given day, the fund or unit trust group will be happy to tell you the buying and selling price of your units or shares (when you buy a fund, you own shares; when you purchase a UIT, you own units).

Finding out the value of your individual bonds is a little more difficult. Your broker or advisor can certainly do the legwork for you, or you can look in the newspaper. Since only a small number of bonds are tracked daily in the *Wall Street Journal*, the easiest way for you to gauge how your bond portfolio is doing is to see how the benchmark U.S. government bond is doing. There are actually three benchmark government bond figures: five-, 10- and 30-year bonds. The 10-year bond is the most often quoted in newspapers and on television reports.

Many newspapers cover a very small number of municipal issues. By seeing how these bonds are doing, you will have a good idea as to how you are doing.

TAX CONSIDERATIONS

When you own a bond, there are two tax considerations: (1) taxation of interest and (2) gains or losses that result from the sale of the security. Outside a qualified retirement plan or variable annuity, there is no way to avoid such current taxation. Interest from direct obligations of the U.S. government (Treasury bills, notes, and bonds, plus Series EE and Series HH bonds) are exempt from state and local income taxes but not from federal income taxes. Interest received from minus is exempt from federal income taxes. If you own a bond that was issued in your state of residence, it is also exempt from any state and local taxes. The only exceptions to this exemption are "private issue" bonds (securities issued by the private sector or a corporation) and a few states that tax certain municipal bonds issued within their state. Private issue bonds are rare, and instances of a state not recognizing the tax-exempt status of some of its issues is even rarer. Still, to be on the safe side, always ask your broker if the interest from the bond you are thinking of buying is free from state *and* federal income taxes.

The second tax consideration is what happens when you sell or redeem a bond for a price that is different from what you paid for it. After all, you may buy a bond for $930 and later sell it for $1,000. Conversely, if you pay $1,300 for a bond and sell it for $850, there is a loss. A sale price that is different from the purchase price means that a taxable event has been triggered. In the case of municipal bonds, the interest income remains tax free; it is the proceeds from the sale that cause a tax event. If you sell or redeem a bond for more than you paid for it, it is a capital gain; if the proceeds are less than the original purchase price, it is a capital loss. Gains or losses must be reported on your tax return for the calendar year in which the bonds were sold. Appreciation or depreciation is not taxable until the bonds are actually sold.

Many people are under the mistaken impression that everything about municipal bonds is tax free. As just described, this is only true with the interest payments. Still, ever since 1986, when many tax schemes and shelters were eliminated, minus remain one of the few "tax shelters," and in some respects, the only true form of tax-free income.

ARE BONDS RIGHT FOR YOU?

How bonds fit into your portfolio depends upon your risk level and the amount of time you are considering. If your time horizon is only a couple of years, then your portfolio should be heavily weighted toward bonds, even if you are a fairly aggressive investor.

For most people, stocks are a better choice than bonds. Bonds have a high degree of predictability, which is good, but have not been considered a good hedge against inflation. Even when you are in your mid-60s, it is the cumulative effects of inflation that will be scarier than the long-term ups and downs of the stock market.

Bonds can help reduce portfolio risk, unlike most kinds of stocks. Whenever possible, make whatever commitment you have to bonds inside a sheltered vehicle such as a variable annuity or qualified retirement plan. Tax-free bonds should be held outside of a retirement account, and, depending upon your comfort level, make domestic quality bonds as small a part of your portfolio as possible.

For municipal bonds, the decision as to whether you should own individual issues, a unit trust, or a fund depends upon your particular circumstances. If you think that your tax bracket may be lower in the future, you should probably lean toward a fund (you could later switch into a government or corporate bond fund by making one telephone call). If professional, ongoing management is important, then funds and unit trusts should be looked at (funds do have more active management, but problems with unit trusts are minuscule). If you feel interest rates are going to go down and you want to sell your bonds at a profit, than you will see your greatest appreciation with individual issues.

Municipal bonds are an attractive addition to a wide range of portfolios. The tax-free interest coupled with reduced volatility makes them a solid choice. For the aggressive investor, it is a way to tone down the overall volatility of a portfolio. For the moderate investor, it is a way of seeing growth through the reinvestment of tax-free interest payments. For the conservative investor, minus provide a reliable source of income that doesn't go up or down.

If you're not an active investor, you're better off with a unit trust or fund. These portfolios are professionally managed. When you own an individual bond, there is always the chance that it will be called away, increase or decrease in value, or have its rating changed without your immediate knowledge. Individual bonds are probably best for the investor who wants a specific maturity date.

Many investors at or near retirement find minus to be a worry-free investment. As you can now see, their beliefs are well founded.

CHAPTER 9

High-Yield Bonds

Why high-yield bond funds are not as risky as they sound—
and why they make a great choice as part of a balanced portfolio

HIGH-YIELD BOND BASICS

Of all the bond categories, high-yield is, overall, the best. High-yield bonds, also sometimes incorrectly referred to as "junk" bonds, have changed their characteristics over the years. But even before these changes, when junk bonds and high-yield bonds were considered to be synonymous, the category was still superior.

Bonds are issued by corporations in order to raise money. Virtually any corporation can issue bonds. Rating services (such as Moody's or Standard & Poor's) evaluate the current and projected financial stability of these companies. Their bond ratings range from AAA (for the highest quality) to D (for "in default"). Some bonds are not rated, simply because the issuing corporation or municipality is not willing to pay the rating service fee, which can cost tens of thousands of dollars.

The rating is one of the biggest factors in determining how many buyers will be interested in the issue. Poorly rated bonds appeal to a much smaller, more aggressive investor base. Since there is less demand for these securities, the issuing corporations must enhance their yields to attract buyers. The resulting yields, also known as coupon rates, are anywhere from two to six percentage points higher than corporate bonds that are considered extremely safe (i.e., 9% vs. 6%).

The investor receives interest income from these bonds as long as he or she owns them. If the bonds are sold prior to their maturity, the sale price may be more or less than what was originally paid for the securities. If the bonds are held until maturity, the issuer will pay the holder full face value. This, by the way, is true with all bonds, including government and municipal.

If the issuing corporations were more financially secure and/or had been around longer, they would issue investment grade, also known as bank-quality, bonds. Bonds that are not rated investment grade are often referred to as high-yield or junk. These are securities with a rating of less than BAA (if you were using the Moody's rating system) or BBB (if you were using Standard & Poor's). Since the great majority of corporations in America (nearly 90%) do not have the financial clout to issue bond ratings of AAA, AA, A, or BBB, they are forced to issue high-yield bonds. Investors, of course, are attracted to high-yield bonds because of their better-than-average rate of return.

In reality, there is a big difference between junk and high-yield bonds, even though the terms high-yield and junk are frequently used interchangeably. Junk bonds are those debt instruments used for corporate takeovers (trying to buy another company with paper instead of sweat, hard work, and cash). High-yield bonds really represent those securities that have had a long track record of overall reliability for the timely payment of interest and principal; they also represent those bonds that have had comparatively few defaults.

A high-yield corporate bond fund, within the context of this book, is simply a mutual fund whose objective is high current income—while keeping an eye on preserving principal. These are the funds that are willing to sacrifice a little bit of current income (i.e., accepting say 8% instead of 10% to 12% current income) in return for having bonds that are at the high end of the junk bond spectrum (e.g., B- or BB-rated bonds instead of CCC-, CC- or C-rated securities).

The only really unique thing about junk bonds is how they are perceived by the public: high return but also high risk. In reality, high-yield bond funds can deliver a wide range of current income, quality, and total return. You cannot condemn the entire stock market because some stocks went down last week or last year, and the same holds true for the high-yield bond market. The fact is that these bonds can provide valuable additional income for individuals and couples who rely on their investments to supplement their income.

On a similar note, it is wrong to think that the world of bonds is black and white, that a security is either investment grade (bank quality) or junk. The reality is, as with other things in life, that there are several shades of gray. Some of those shades of gray can translate into a safe investment that is a diamond in the rough.

High-Quality Corporate Bonds

The only thing special about corporate bonds is that you have lent money to a specific corporation. If you own part of a unit trust or shares in a bond fund, then you have loaned money to a large number of companies. In return for the use of your money, the corporation agrees to pay you (or the unit trust or mutual fund) interest every six months. When the bond matures, the issuer further promises to pay back the face value of the bond. The face value may be more or less than what you paid for the bond. Corporate bonds are redeemed for $1,000 each at maturity. If you paid more than $1,000 for the bond, you will experience a "loss" at maturity. Conversely, if you paid less than $1,000, you will have a capital gain upon redemption.

I said "loss" in the previous paragraph because bonds are often bought at a premium in order to get a higher current yield. The higher income every six months can end up easily offsetting any "loss" at maturity. Oftentimes, it is better to have more now and accept a little bit less later (what is known as the time value of money).

When a corporation issues bonds, it must decide whether or not to have the security rated. A good rating will make the bond more marketable and, therefore, more desirable. A corporation may decide not to have its issue(s) rated for one or more of the following reasons: (1) The corporation has a high degree of certainty that the rating will be poor (and there is no reason to pay for something that will make your bond more difficult to sell). (2) The fee charged by the rating service, which can be $10,000 to $20,000 or more, may be too high in light of the face value of the outstanding bonds (it does not make sense to pay, say, $20,000 for a $1.5 million dollar issue). (3) The track record of the corporation, and its outstanding bonds, may be so well known that there are several buyers who are willing to buy the debt with or without a rating.

There are several rating services, but, as a general rule, ratings are based on the following: (1) the corporation's ability to pay its current debts, (2) trends in sales and profit margins, (3) the caliber of management and its efficiency, (4) the corporation's position compared with its competitors in the same industry, (5) the outlook of the entire industry, and (6) the projected growth, costs, profits, and so forth, of the corporation. The rating decision is mostly objective. Once a rating has been given, the corporation is always free to pay another fee to have the same, or another, rating service make a new analysis.

Corporations strive for a high rating because the interest paid out by the company (a cost of doing business) can amount to a large percentage of its overall expenses. A higher rating means that the company will pay less in interest if it issues new bonds in the future. A difference of one or two percentage points can end up saving, or costing, the corporation hundreds of thousands of dollars per year. The figure could turn out to be millions if the debt about to be issued amounts to a couple of hundred million dollars.

Its rating distinguishes a high quality bond from other types of corporate bonds. The two major rating services, Moody's and Standard & Poor's, consider the top four categories (AAA, AA, A, and BAA in the case of Moody's; AAA, AA, A, and BBB in the case of Standard & Poor's) to be high-quality. The higher the rating, the more likely the corporation will be able to meet its current and future debt obligations. Similarly, the higher the rating, the lower the risk and the lower the yield. As the chance for default or suspension in interest payments decreases, so does the risk. The default rate for high-quality corporate bonds is a small fraction of 1%.

The rating of a bond can change over time. A financially strong corporation can fall on bad times and have the rating on its outstanding debt downgraded by any of the rating services. A downgrading (e.g., A to BAA) or boost (e.g., AA to AAA) may last for only several months or indefinitely. It is the rating services that decide what rating a corporation's bonds will receive; the issuer has no control and cannot influence the rating service.

Once you buy a bond, its coupon rate (the amount of interest paid out by the corporation) is fixed. Thus, a corporation does not benefit, nor is it harmed, by a change in ratings, as far as its existing (outstanding) debt is concerned. A higher rating could benefit the corporation in the future and probably reflect favorably on senior management as well as the board of directors. A company that is considered to be sound financially has more latitude when it comes to dealing with creditors, vendors, and employees. People like dealing with safe companies. No one likes to buy a product or service from a business that appears to be troubled and may only survive for a few more years.

ADVANTAGES OF OWNING HIGH-YIELD BONDS

There are two advantages to high-yield bonds: a better current return and reduced volatility most of the time. As already mentioned, people who buy these securities expect something extra for taking on more financial risk. Financial risk refers to the possibility that the corporation may go into bankruptcy, foreclosure, or reorganization. As scary as this sounds, only 2% or 3% of the outstanding corporate bond market experiences such troubles most years. Equally important, those that do often are able to turn around and show a profit as well as pay off all bondholders.

The second advantage, reduced interest-rate volatility, has already been described in a previous chapter that dealt with bonds. Briefly, lower fluctuations in value are beneficial to an investor who may want to sell his or her bonds prior to their maturity. If your underlying principal does not go up or down very much in value, there is a greater chance that you will be made whole at the time of sale. Volatility, however, is a two-way street. When interest rates are falling, and bond prices are going up, you will have wished that you owned these types of bonds. It is only when rates are increasing that you want to own more stable interest-rate securities.

With high-yield bond funds you also have the advantage of ongoing, professional management (that can get rid of a bond before it becomes greatly troubled), reduced risk (since you own part of a very diversified portfolio), and the ability to switch among other funds within the same family with a simple phone call. The price per share (value) of high-yield bond funds is reported in the mutual fund section of the newspaper each day.

The advantage of buying a high-quality corporate bond is peace of mind. By buying a safe corporate bond you get a return that is 1% to 2% higher than a U.S. government obligation that has a similar maturity. Like other types of bonds, high-quality issues pay interest semiannually. And, like other bonds, if interest rates decline from the time when you purchased your bonds, their value increases.

DISADVANTAGES TO OWNING HIGH-YIELD BONDS

There are also two disadvantages to high-yield bonds: credit, or financial, risk and price changes during poor or uncertain economic periods. Since the financial, or credit, risk of these bonds has already been discussed, this section focuses on price changes.

When the U.S. economy is going through the initial or middle stages of a recession, high-yield bonds may drop in value. This is because there is a perceived, and sometimes real, concern that corporations that are not among the strongest in financial terms will default on their obligations. During the later stages of a recession, junk bonds can experience tremendous gains. For example, some high-yield corporate bond funds were up over 40% for 1991, easily beating out all other types of bond funds and even outperforming several categories of stock funds.

The biggest disadvantage of owning high-quality corporate bonds is that their rating can go down, thereby decreasing the value if the bond is sold prior to its natural maturity. True, the rating may also go up, but when you have a bond that is already A or AA rated, its safety can only go up a little bit, whereas the potential fall could be severe. Fortunately, rating adjustments are more the exception than the rule. Furthermore, the chances that a bond's rating will drop by two or more grades are extremely small.

RISK AND RETURN

As you might suspect, the biggest risk with high-yield bonds is the risk of default. No one likes to own a bond that has stopped or suspended paying interest. More importantly, no one likes to have their principal in jeopardy of not being paid back. As mentioned previously, the number of junk bonds that default is very small compared with the thousands that perform just fine. Losses from defaults are rarely one hundred cents on the dollar. At least one study shows that investors get back approximately 70 cents on the dollar when this worst-case situation occurs.

To reduce the chances of default even further, investors should use a mutual fund or variable annuity subaccount. With such professional management and ongoing supervision, the risk of default should fall into the one half of 1% range.

The public, as well as uninformed brokers and advisors, has the belief that high-yield bonds are riskier than government or high-quality corporate issues. Risk comes in several forms, and when it comes to bonds, the three greatest risks are default, interest rate, and purchasing power. Since high-yield bonds have had a higher return than government, municipal, or high-quality corporate bonds, this also means that they have less purchasing power risk. Phrased another way, high-yield bonds have been a better hedge against inflation over the past 20 years.

Interest-rate risk refers to what happens to the underlying value of a bond when interest rates move up or down. When interest rates change (or there is fear or excitement about a change), a bond's volatility is determined by its maturity and its yield. The longer the maturity, the greater the volatility; the higher the yield, the more insensitive or stable the bond's value becomes.

Since high-yield bonds have a greater yield than other kinds of domestic bonds, as well as typically shorter maturity, they possess less interest-rate risk than government, municipal, or high-quality corporate debt instruments—even when such instruments have the same maturity.

The final, and most important, form of risk associated with a bond is the risk of default. U.S. government bonds have no default risk. Municipal bonds, as a general category, are also very safe—second in safety only to government bonds. High-quality corporate bonds also almost never default. High-yield bonds, on the other hand, do have a default risk. However, the risk of default has fallen to about 2% a year over the past few years. In a typical mutual fund or variable annuity subaccount, the risk of default falls to about one quarter or one half of 1%. This, by the way, is where the distinction between junk bonds and high-yield bonds becomes important.

Junk bonds, which have a rating of CCC, CC, C, or even lower, offer current yields that are typically two to four points higher than high-yield bonds, which have a rating of BBB, BB, or B. When it comes to mutual funds or variable annuity subaccounts, you can tell whether the fund is junk or high-yield oriented by its current yield. If the yield of portfolio X is a couple of points higher than other such bond portfolios, it is almost a guarantee that it is a much riskier portfolio and should be avoided by most investors. When it comes to high-yield bonds, it is better to take a little less current yield (but still at least a couple of points higher than government bonds) in return for greater interest-rate stability of principal and often a higher total return figure (meaning greater potential for appreciation of principal).

The biggest risk involved in owning high-quality corporate bonds is that you will sell them before they mature and when interest rates are higher than they were at the time of purchase. Since the rating is good, the chance of default is virtually nil.

BUYING AND SELLING HIGH-YIELD BONDS

You buy and sell junk bonds just the way you would any other type of bond: individually, in a bond fund, or as part of a unit trust. Mutual funds and unit trusts that are heavily loaded with junk issues are usually easy to spot because of their name. Names such as the XYZ High-Yield Bond Fund or the ABC Enhanced Return Unit Trust often translate into "We own at least a moderate amount, if not a lot, of lower-rated securities."

Investors who buy individual high-yield bonds should do so only if they are intimately familiar with the issuing corporation or are willing to keep on top of the financial news. Otherwise, stick with funds and unit trusts. These organizations are staffed with people who understand the workings of this marketplace and often know what is a good buy and what should be dumped. When you compare and contrast funds and unit trusts, do not be tempted by higher than expected current yields. Look at total return figures for each of the last several years. By factoring in the value of the underlying bonds, you will quickly be able to see which funds and trusts are stocked with good quality junk and have very poorly rated issues (but capture investors by advertising a very high current income or yield).

Even though high-yield bonds are not as popular as high-quality securities, they can still be bought or sold within a few minutes. Like other bonds, junk bonds are most commonly traded in increments of five (e.g., a face value of

$5000, $10,000, $15,000, etc.). Thus, when you buy a bond, you must normally purchase or sell five, 10, 15, and so on, at a time.

Buying And Selling High-Quality Corporate Bonds

High-quality corporate issues can be bought or sold through a securities firm, financial planner, or investment advisor. Several banks also offer similar brokerage services. A great number of mutual fund groups have high-quality portfolios that can be purchased or sold with a phone call. Unit trusts are still another alternate form of ownership.

It takes only a couple of minutes to buy or sell individual bonds, a unit trust, or shares of a high-quality corporate bond fund. The price is determined by the general level of interest rates.

You can buy high-quality corporate bonds that have maturities ranging from a few months to 30 years. Usually, the longer the maturity, the greater the yield (since such bonds are more volatile). A high-quality bond is not immune from interest rate swings. When rates go up, all bonds, even those issued by the U.S. government, will go down in value; how much they decline depends upon how much interest rates have risen and the remaining maturity of the bond (e.g., a 30-year bond issued 25 years ago is no more volatile than a five-year bond issued yesterday).

TAX CONSIDERATIONS

The interest received from high-yield corporate bonds, whether through individual issues, a mutual fund, or a unit trust, is fully taxable in the year in which it is received. You will receive a Form 1099 from the issuer, fund, or trust each year; reinvestment of interest payments or some other diversion will not mitigate the taxation of corporate or government bond interest.

As mentioned previously, there is also the issue of capital gains and capital losses. If the bonds are sold for a profit (more than you paid for them, minus any accrued interest), this results in a capital gain. If the sale proceeds are less than your purchase price, there is a capital loss. Capital losses offset capital gains, dollar for dollar. Thus, if you sell ABC stock for a $70,000 gain and you also sell XYZ bonds for a $40,000 loss and JKL bonds for a $10,000 loss, you will only have to pay taxes on $20,000 ($70K minus $40K minus $10K).

Interest from corporate bonds is fully taxable on a state and a federal level. The interest is taxable in the year in which it is received or reinvested. Corporations, mutual funds, and unit trusts all issue Form 1099s, so make sure that you report all of the interest received or reinvested.

The only way to avoid taxation of corporate bond interest is to buy such securities within a retirement plan such as an IRA or pension plan. If you have children, you can make a gift of the bonds to the children and the interest will be taxed under their income bracket, up to a certain level. After the first $1,400 (for 2001) of unearned income (i.e., dividends, interest payments, capital gains, etc.), taxes are based on the income bracket of the child's parents, even if the bonds were gifted by a relative or friend. Once the child reaches age 14, all earned and unearned income is taxed at the child's rate, which is frequently zero percent.

Besides interest, there is the issue of capital gains or losses. Any such gain or loss must be reported on your tax return. If you sell or redeem a bond for exactly the same price you paid for it, there is no taxable capital gain or loss.

ARE HIGH-YIELD BONDS RIGHT FOR YOU?

Bonds are an important part of one's holdings. Often, they can add a great deal of stability when the stock or real estate markets are uncertain. It is very uncommon for both high-quality bonds and stocks to decline in value the same year.

Since junk bonds throw off a substantial amount of current income, they are most effectively used, taxwise, in a qualified retirement plan or in a variable annuity. They are also appropriate for investors who are in a low tax bracket and may or may not be able to shelter such income.

The second issue concerning portfolio fit involves the patience and risk tolerance of the investor. If you are ultraconservative, you should avoid junk bonds. If, on a scale of one to ten, you are a two through seven (the higher the number, the higher the risk), then you should look at high-yield bonds and have them comprise up to 15% of your portfolio. Someone above a "seven" will not find high-yield bonds exciting enough (unless we experience another 1991).

High-yield bonds perform best and are certainly more stable if they are held for at least five years. Such a holding period helps to amortize any future disasters, such as the ones experienced in 1989 and 1990. However, it is very doubtful that these bonds will go through such severe losses in the future. Now that the marketplace has seen what can happen to junk bonds, it is likely to learn from its past excesses and weed out those issues that are based on rosy predictions.

One of the nice features of high-quality corporate bonds is that they pay interest whether or not the economy, real estate, or stock market are performing well. If you own part of a unit trust or individual bonds, your yield will not fluctuate. You receive, or reinvest, the same amount every six months (every month if you are in a unit trust). High quality issues provide a reliable source of income. The increase or decrease in value referred to throughout this chapter is of greatest importance to someone who plans on selling their bonds prior to his or her maturity.

We all know that the world is not full of absolutes. Not every stockbroker is just a salesperson, not every doctor is rich, and not every lawyer is smart. The same is true with the world of investments. Historically, stocks have been a great investment, but there are hundreds of equities that have lost money over the past decade. Few people in California ever thought real estate prices could actually go down. Junk bonds sound risky and many of them are; however, this does not mean that certain categories of junk are not safe and a good deal.

A good investment is just like a good marriage or relationship: It takes work. In the case of investing, you must do your homework. Do not automatically exclude high-yield bonds just because of the bad publicity they received a few years ago. What the press never told you was that well over 95% of these bonds have never been in trouble. Besides, if you relied on yesterday's news, you would have missed out on stocks in the 1980s and 1990s, and probably will never buy CDs or government bonds again because they are not particularly attractive right now. As more than one famous, and rich, investor has said in the past, "Buy when everyone else is selling."

Many investors may be better served by owning U.S. government bonds than by buying high-quality bonds. Since there is usually little difference between the yield on similar maturing government and high-quality corporate bonds, take the safer investment. With government securities you never have to worry about a downgrading, payment of interest, or repayment of principal. Equally important, during periods of panic, when the marketplace temporarily believes in world disaster, government issues will increase in value, as people flock to quality.

CHAPTER 10

The Right Mix

*How to choose the best combination of
stocks, bonds, and cash for your portfolio*

SHOULD YOU HANDLE YOUR OWN FINANCIAL PLANNING?

The financial services community would like you to believe that you are completely dependent on their financial planning talents. The "experts" will assure you that they—and not you—should be responsible for your investment and estate planning needs. What they will not tell you is that the conflicts of interest inherent in trying to make their own business more successful can easily cloud their judgment and advice. What they will also fail to mention is that certain parts of investing and planning must really be done by you—and no one else.

A lot of people think that they know everything they need to know after attending a few classes or reading a couple of books or subscribing to a magazine about investing. These sources of information should be telling you that this attitude may be true some of the time—but only in isolated circumstances or with certain specific investments. Instead, they preserve their subscription base by telling you that you are perfectly capable of handling the entire investment process on your own.

The point is that every business is a business. True, you and I could learn how to fix our car, repair our plumbing, or dispense simple medical advice after reading a couple of books or attending a few seminars. However, we would never be a match for the electrician or stockbroker who spends 8 to 12 hours a day practicing his or her craft. You should have a certain degree of knowledge so that you won't be taken advantage of, but no one can be a "jack of all trades." A respectable level of knowledge is a form of protection and may help ensure that the person you hire is not neglectful or negligent.

The aspects of financial planning that you can, and should, do on your own include the following:

1. Have an understanding of basic financial planning.
2. Use a discount broker for certain securities.
3. Research certain qualities and features of mutual funds.
4. Get comparison quotes for insurance.
5. Negotiate some of the costs associated with investing.
6. Avoid "packaged" or "professionally managed" investments for certain securities.

Planning is Essential

There is a saying that no one will watch over your investments as carefully as you will. This is true, but such scrutiny has its price. Watching over an investment or portfolio on a daily or even weekly basis can result in unnecessary anxiety and possibly poor investment decisions.

Throughout our lives, we are confronted with instructions, directions, procedure manuals, warnings, and advice. We may not like to admit it, but these plans are a necessary part of our everyday life.

Yet, when it comes to financial planning, many people act as though there shouldn't be a plan. I don't know whether it's because the subject can be confusing, or because people are just reluctant to talk about it, or because in many cases, investment programs can seem pretty abstract. But, just like other aspects of your everyday life, planning for your future is not something that you should take lightly. In short, you will get to where you want to go if you have a plan, a set of instructions, a little sound advice, and a few warnings.

Over 90 percent of all Americans have no idea where their investments or pension will take them. They don't know how long they can count on their sources of income, how much money their investments will produce over time, or how much financial risk they are exposed to. In short, they have no financial plan.

A financial plan gives us a framework within which we can look for investment opportunities. With a plan that reflects our goals and resources, we can map out where we are and calculate where we can expect to end up.

A good battle plan also takes the enemy into account. In the case of financial planning, there are three enemies: inflation, taxes, and procrastination.

This chapter shows you how to draft your own financial plan. This doesn't mean that you can skip consulting an investment advisor. The objectivity and experience a good financial planner can bring to the table have tremendous value. However, by drafting your own financial plan, you will gain greater knowledge of your assets—information that will make your investment and strategy meetings more meaningful.

A SAMPLE FINANCIAL PLAN

The best way to see how a financial plan is constructed is to go through an example. As you read through this example, try to ignore the fact that the particulars of this hypothetical illustration do not coincide with your age, current holdings, time horizon, and so on. The important thing to understand is *how* the process works. When you finish reading the example, you should be able to draft your own personal plan.

Assume the following investor profile:

1. Goal: to retire comfortably in 20 years
2. Objective: to end up with a portfolio that will produce $3,000 a month in income
3. Current holdings (income and growth to be reinvested):
   - $50,000 in bank CDs averaging 8%
   - $40,000 in tax-free bonds that yield 7%
   - $30,000 in a mutual fund that averages 12% growth
   - $7,000 (each year) that can be invested in a company retirement plan that averages a 14% return
4. Expectation: that inflation will average 5% over the next 20 years
5. Tax bracket: 35% (state and federal combined)
6. Risk level: moderate

The investor wants to know what he or she can expect to have at the end of 20 years (upon retirement). The best way to solve this problem is to look at each individual investment and project its future value at the end of 20 years. Our projections take into account the investor's existing holdings, the amount that can be saved each year, the tax bracket, the expected rate of inflation, and the projected rate of return. The value of each asset is then added up, to calculate the total final portfolio value.

$50,000 in Bank CDs

The CD money is expected to grow at an 8% compound annual rate over the next 20 years. First we need to adjust this figure for income taxes and inflation. From the following steps, you can see what the after-tax, after-inflation rate of return is for this investment:

Expected rate of return	*8%*
Minus income taxes *(35% of 8% equals 2.8%)*	*– 3%*
Equals the after-tax return	*5%*
Minus the rate of inflation	*– 5%*
Equals the real rate of return	*0%*

As you can see, once inflation and taxes are factored in, this particular investment will not grow.

$40,000 in Municipal Bonds

The tax-free bonds are expected to grow at a 7% compound annual rate over the next 20 years. Again, we need to adjust this figure for inflation. No adjustment is needed for income taxes since the interest from this investment is tax free. However, just because something is sheltered from income taxes does not mean that it escapes the effects of inflation. From the following steps, you can see what the after-tax, after-inflation rate of return is for this investment:

Expected rate of return	*7%*
Minus income taxes *(interest from municipal bonds is tax free)*	*– 0%*
Equals the after-tax return	*7%*
Minus the rate of inflation	*– 5%*
Equals the real rate of return	*2%*

As you can see, this hypothetical investment will grow at a real rate of 2% over the next 20 years, assuming the rate of return, income tax bracket, and level of inflation previously noted. An investment of $40,000 earning interest at a real rate of return of 2% will grow to $59,600 over the next 20 years.

$30,000 in a Mutual Fund

The mutual fund is projected to grow at a 12% compound annual rate over the next 20 years. Again, we need to adjust this figure for income taxes and inflation. From the following steps, you can see what the real rate of return is for this investment:

Expected rate of return	*12%*
Minus income taxes *(35% of 12% equals 4.2%)*	*– 4%*
Equals the after-tax return	*8%*
Minus the rate of inflation	*– 5%*
Equals the real rate of return	*3%*

As you can see, this particular investment will grow at a real rate of 3% over the next 20 years. An investment of $30,000 will grow to $54,300 over the next 20 years, assuming a real rate of return of 3%.

$7,000 That Can Be Saved Each Year

Finally, the investor feels he or she can save $7,000 each year to be earmarked for a retirement plan. This plan has historically averaged 14% compounded annually. Once again, we need to adjust this figure for inflation. Monies invested in a qualified retirement plan grow and compound tax-deferred. From the following steps, you can see what the after-inflation rate of return is for this investment:

Expected rate of return	*14%*
Minus income taxes *(tax-deferred growth, no current taxation)*	*– 0%*
Equals the after-tax return	*14%*
Minus the rate of inflation	*– 5%*
Equals the real rate of return	*9%*

As you can see, this particular investment will grow at a real rate of 9% over the next 20 years. An investment of $7,000 set aside each year will grow to $358,120 over the next 20 years, assuming a real rate of return of 9%.

The following list shows how our hypothetical investor's investments have prepared him or her for retirement. (All figures represent the real rate of growth.)

ORIGINAL INVESTMENT	GROWS TO
$50,000 in bank CDs	$50,000
$40,000 in tax-free bonds	$59,600
$30,000 in a mutual fund	$54,300
$7,000 saved each year	$358,120
Total of all investments	$522,020

If the entire $522,020 is invested in 9% corporate bonds at retirement, the investor will have an annual income of $48,998 (9% of $522,020), well in excess of the investor's $36,000 annual goal. Even better results could be obtained by broader diversification.

Now that you have gone through a sample plan, it's time to apply what you have learned to your own particular situation. The next section shows you how to draft your own investment plan, taking into account your goals, objectives, existing holdings, and tax bracket, as well as your feelings about risk and your projections regarding inflation.

DRAFTING YOUR OWN PLAN

An investment plan comprises five parts: goals, objectives, strategy, implementation, and performance. The following sections take a closer look at these five components.

Goals

Each of us has goals we would like to attain. For most people, the chief financial goal is to "retire comfortably." Some individuals and couples have multiple goals, such as to send their children through college, and to travel abroad once every three years. Whatever your goals are, you have a good chance of obtaining them all, with proper planning.

Step one of your financial plan is to list your goals. On the following lines, list, in order of priority, your three most important financial goals:

1. _____

2. _____

3. _____

Objectives

Once your goals are listed, you need to determine what it will take to "buy" those goals. Therefore, you must turn those goals into dollar objectives. For example, if your major goal is to retire comfortably, that might translate into building a nest egg that will produce $6,000 of income every month. A "comfortable retirement" for another individual or couple might be $2,000 per month, or maybe even just $800 per month. We all have different dreams and lifestyles. The important thing is to list the dollar figures that ensure that your goals will be fulfilled. Before you figure out those dollar figures, a little math review is in order.

Math Review

Suppose that you have decided your chief goal is to retire comfortably. You have further decided that in your particular case, a comfortable retirement requires $6,000 of income per month, after taxes. You now know the solution to the equation, but there are still some blanks to fill in. Specifically, you need to know how much principal must be accumulated to produce $6,000 per month, along with a reasonable rate of return that can be expected from this lump sum.

As of this writing, a conservative investor could purchase high-quality municipal bonds that offered a current yield of 4%. When you decide to start securing your goals and objectives, municipal (also known as tax-free) bonds might be yielding anywhere from 3% to 11%. The precise rate is not important; what is important is that you understand how to solve the problem.

For the sake of our example, assume that tax-free bonds have a current yield of 4%. (I'm using tax-free bonds in this example because they are a conservative investment that is very popular with retirees.) You need to project a specific rate of return to complete these calculations, and even at these initial stages, you need to assume a specific rate of return to help determine the size of the lump sum you need to achieve your objective. Follow these three steps:

1. Take the desired monthly income figure, $6,000 in this example, and multiply it by the 12 months of the year. The resulting figure, $72,000 ($6,000 times 12 months), is what you want to end up with on an annual basis.

2. To determine how much you must initially invest to have a return of $6,000 per month, take the annual figure, $72,000 in this example, and divide it by the projected tax-free rate (or whatever investment you wish to use) of return at retirement. In this example, assume that you can get a 4% yield from a municipal bond.

3. The lump-sum figure you need, the result of dividing $72,000 by .04, is $1,800,000. By investing a lump sum of $1,800,000 in long-term, tax-free municipal bonds yielding 4% annually, you will end up with $6,000 per month of income ($1,800,000 times .04 equals $72,000; $72,000 divided by the 12 months of the year equals $6,000 per month).

Therefore, your chief goal is to end up with $1,800,000 at retirement. Add in two other goals: sending two children through college and buying a new car every four years. After doing a little bit of research on the costs of these goals, you can translate them into dollar figures, using today's dollars.

OBJECTIVES	GOALS
Retire comfortably	$1,800,000
College education	$250,000
Buy a new car	$20,000
Total	$2,070,000

Make sure that you list your goals in order of priority. If things don't work out as planned, you want to ensure that you end up at least obtaining your top one or two objectives.

As you can see, these are all lump-sum figures. Now that you have arrived at your goals and translated them into dollar figures, you must figure out how much money you will have to save each year to end up with the desired lump sums. Presumably, these annual savings will not be sitting around idle; they will be invested in some type of investment. The specific investments and their expected rates of return are discussed in the next section.

Strategy

Before figuring out how much you will need to save each year to reach the dollar objectives listed (retirement, college, and new cars), take inventory of any existing holdings. For the purposes of this example, assume that you already own the following assets:

1. $250,000 in high-yield corporate bonds yielding 9%
2. $200,000 in a pension plan that grows at 10%
3. $30,000 that can be saved every year

To further elaborate on the example, assume that it will be 20 years until you retire, that you are in a 33% tax bracket (state and federal combined), and that the inflation rate will be 5%. Tuition costs will begin in ten years, and you would like to buy a new car every four years.

Getting back to the example, $250,000 in corporate bonds will grow at 9% before taxes, but only at 6% once taxes are subtracted. (If you begin with a 9% return and a third [3%] is taken away in taxes [a 33% state and federal tax bracket], you end up with 6%.) A 6% return, reduced by the rate of inflation, 5% in our example, ends up with a real rate of return of 1%. Thus, $250,000 grows to only $305,000 in 20 years at a real rate of return of 1%.

You also have, hypothetically, $200,000 in a pension plan that has been averaging 10% annually over the past few years. Let us see what you will end up with if this rate continues for the next 20 years. A 10% return, minus 5% for inflation, leaves you with a 5% growth rate. Notice two things here. First, income taxes have not been taken out; money in a retirement plan grows and compounds tax-deferred. You will deal with income taxes only as withdrawals are made. Second, just because something is sheltered from taxes does not mean that it is also being shielded from inflation. Inflation affects the true rate of return of every investment, whether it is fully taxable, tax-deferred, or tax free. There is no hiding from the cumulative effects of inflation. Going back to the example, at a 5% after-inflation rate of return for 20 years, $200,000 grows to $530,000.

We have one more source of investment left in our example: the $30,000 that can be saved each year until retirement. Assume that you will invest this money in high-yield tax-free municipal bonds. And suppose that over the next 20 years you will average a 7% yield on these bonds. If you start with a 7% tax-free yield and subtract income taxes, you still end up with 7% (since no income tax is due on the interest from municipal bonds). The 7% after-tax return is still affected by inflation. Therefore, take 7% and subtract the assumed rate of inflation, 5%, over the next 20 years. This leaves you with a 2% real rate of return annually. Thus, $30,000 saved annually at a 2% real rate of return will increase to $690,000 in 20 years.

The growth rate, or final value of the original assets, plus annual savings, can now be determined as follows:

ORIGINAL INVESTMENT	GROWS TO
$250,000	$305,000
$200,000	$530,000
$30,000 saved each year	$690,000
Total	$1,525,000

As you can see, the existing investments will not satisfy your retirement goal. The retirement goal alone meant that $1,800,000 needed to be acquired at the end of 20 years. You are close to a $300,000 short of your first goal. A decision needs to be made at this point. You will need to cut back on your goal of $6,000 per month at retirement, be more aggressive in your investment plan, and/or reduce or completely eliminate your final two goals.

Plan B

In the preceding example, your hypothetical investment program fell far short of your goals. In order to reach all or most of these goals, some part of your investment program has to be changed.

As an investor, you can do one of the following: (1) reposition your investments to take advantage of higher rates of return and/or growth, (2) save more money each year, (3) retire later than expected, or (4) lower your retirement expectations. The following sections explore these options.

Reposition Your Investments

The least painful alternative is to look for alternative investments that would produce a higher return. By evaluating their after-tax rate of return and taking on just a little more risk, investors can usually better their returns dramatically.

First, you should try to shelter as many of your holdings from taxes as possible. Sheltering means that you are turning an asset that is fully taxable into an investment that is either tax free or tax-deferred. This may not always be a great strategy, for one or more of the following reasons:

1. You may be in a lower tax bracket—so, on an after-tax basis, a tax-free instrument may not produce as high a return as an investment that is fully taxable.
2. You may already have a significant portion of your holdings in municipal bonds, and any addition would result in an under-diversification (adding to your risk).
3. Tax-deferred investments, such as annuities and retirement accounts, cannot be sold before age 59½ without incurring a 10% penalty.
4. Sheltered vehicles may not provide you with the investment options or the specific management company you are looking for.

Municipal bonds and tax-free money market funds are the only investments that provide a truly tax-free rate of return. Tax-free bonds typically yield 2% to 4% more annually than their tax-free money market counterparts.

In the previous example, you could shift the $250,000 in high-yield corporate bonds yielding 9% into 7% high-yield municipal bonds. This would change the after-tax rate of return from 6% (9% gross return minus one third for income taxes) to 7% (since their current yield is tax free). The $250,000 would then be worth $372,500 at the end of 20 years.

Regarding the second investment, you could move the $200,000 in pension plan money into a global stock mutual fund. This type of fund invests in common stocks around the world. The typical global fund has somewhere between 30% and 60% of its assets in U.S. securities; the balance is in foreign stocks. Historically, global funds have averaged returns of 10% to 20% annually. According to a Stanford University study, global funds have 51% less volatility and have experienced much greater returns than U.S. stocks over time. If the $200,000 pension plan averaged 15% annually instead of 10%, the account would be worth $1,346,000 at the end of 20 years (15%, minus 5% for inflation, minus zero for taxes, equals 10%).

Finally, the $30,000 that can be saved every year could be invested in a balanced mutual fund. By choosing a balanced portfolio that is comprised of stocks and bonds, and assuming an average annual rate of return of 12%, the $10,000 of savings each year would grow to $718,000 at the end of 20 years (12% minus 4% for taxes and minus 5% for inflation equals 3%).

The new figures look quite different:

ORIGINAL INVESTMENT	GROWS TO	REPOSTIONED GROWS TO
$250,000	$305,000	$372,500 (repositioned into municipal bonds)
$200,000	$530,000	$1,346,000 (repositioned into global funds)
$30,000 each year	$690,000	$718,000 (repositioned into balanced funds)
Total	$1,525,000	$2,436,500

As you can see, with this reconfiguration you have reached the retirement goal of $1,800,000 just with over $600,000 to spare.

At this point, you may be thinking that since the global funds are the best performing segment of our hypothetical portfolio, you should invest all of your capital in global funds. There are two reasons why this will not work: (1) The reduced volatility, versus purely U.S. stocks, may still be too high for a conservative investor. (2) There is no guarantee global funds or any type of stock-oriented investment will average 10%, 12%, or 15% during the next 10 or 20 years. What we can count on is that a diversified portfolio will include some positive surprises (better than projected returns) and some disappointments (less than expected growth). By combining a range of investments (diversification), the overall return should become more predictable, since the poor performers will be canceled out by the better-than-expected investments.

The second goal is to end up with a lump sum of $250,000 to pay for college education in ten years. The $250,000 that was originally in corporate bonds will certainly meet this goal, even without any real growth. Finally, part of the $30,000 per year that can be saved can now be earmarked for the third goal, a $20,000 new car every four years. Investing $5,000 every year in a balanced fund that has a real rate of return of 3% means that it will grow to $20,900 every four years.

In this example, you reached all of your goals simply by repositioning your assets. But suppose that either this was not enough or that any repositioning would have pushed you into investments that are riskier than you can tolerate— what then? There are only three alternatives: save more each year, postpone your retirement, or lower your expectations.

Save More Each Year

The repositioning suggestions may not appeal to you, either because you have preconceived notions about stocks and bonds or because you have an ultra-conservative approach to investments. It is very difficult for most people to invest in stocks or stock-oriented mutual funds when the stock market has just experienced a crash or "correction." It is hard to get enthusiastic about bonds if, for example, you owned them during the mid-1970s and saw their paper value erode to 50% of face value in less than six years. (Fortunately, they fully recovered this paper loss by the mid- to late 1980s.) If this is the case, you might prefer an alternative—for example, increasing your yearly savings to more than $10,000 each year. A larger annual savings results in a larger final lump-sum amount at retirement.

This alternative may simply not be possible. It may be that you cannot save anything, much less $10,000 annually. Many families either live beyond their means or lack the discipline to save. If this is the case, you can quickly eliminate this alternative.

Postpone Your Retirement

By postponing your retirement, you can give your existing portfolio more time to grow and compound. A $100,000 investment that is sheltered from income taxes and experiences a real growth rate of 8% (after adjusting for inflation) will grow to $200,000 in nine years. The same investment will be worth approximately $300,000 if it is allowed to grow for an additional four years.

Lower Your Expectations

The final alternative is to lower your expectations. Perhaps the kids will have to pay for part of their educational costs. Or maybe you can purchase a new car only every six years instead of every four. You can juggle the numbers, time horizons, and rates of return and end up with a wide range of possibilities.

Implementation and Performance

Once you have decided on a course of action, it is important to implement the plan. Many people think that by doing nothing they somehow protect themselves from investment risks. This is simply not true. There is no "risk-free rate of return" in the real world. Wherever you have invested your money, it is subject to one or more forms of risk. Conservative investments such as Treasury bills, bank CDs, and money market accounts are subjected to income taxes and the cumulative effects of inflation. High-yielding corporate bonds possess the risk of default. Stocks and real estate are subject to market conditions and sometimes wide fluctuations in value.

It is infinitely better to design an investment plan and then follow through on it rather than to maintain the status quo or try to pursue a random assortment of investment "quick fixes." An investment plan will give you something to strive for, a measurable goal that can be calculated, visualized, and reviewed. Without a clear sense of direction, you will end up either chasing the "stock of the month" or being paralyzed by your inability to change out of existing investments that offer poor returns. It has often been said that "those who fail to plan will end up planning to fail."

REVIEW YOUR PROGRESS

No matter how conservative, moderate, or aggressive part or all of your portfolio is, it is important that you review your progress regularly. You should sit down with your investment advisor once or twice a year, and see how each of your investments is performing.

Fundamentally sound investments should not be moved around just because they have experienced a bad quarter or year. If you were to move your money every time a loss was suffered, you would soon end up either broke due to commissions and poor market timing or strictly confined to secure investments such as CDs, money market funds, or T-bills. Remember, these "safe" investments have performed very poorly against inflation on an after-tax basis over the past decades.

After reviewing the portfolio over a period of two or three years, you may decide to become more aggressive or conservative in your approach. This "change of heart" may be due to your age, a change in goals and objectives, unforeseen circumstances, or risk level. Actually experiencing the ups and downs of investments can change your tolerance for risk. Like other life "passages," the experience provides us with familiarity and understanding. This translates into either accepting greater volatility or realizing that you have had enough and are ready to accept your losses and try a different approach. Whatever the reason, most investments can be repositioned easily.

After a few annual reviews, you may be pleasantly surprised to learn that your returns have been better than expected. This means that the final dollar figures may be much higher. You may end up with enough principal at retirement to increase your monthly income by a couple of thousand dollars. It can also mean that perhaps the overall risk level of your portfolio can now be reduced— or that you can retire early! Reducing your risk level could mean exchanging growth mutual funds for balanced funds or high-yield bonds for U.S. government obligations. An earlier retirement means that you may be able to stop working at age 62 instead of 65 or 70. On the other hand, less than expected returns may signal that you need to take a more aggressive or riskier approach to investing, or increase your annual savings.

The major reason for doing a regular review is to make sure that you aren't surprised after too much time has passed and it's too late to change your approach to fit your goals. If you are always aware of just where you stand, you can still achieve your goals and dreams, even if you have made a few mistakes along the way. Successful investment planning includes learning from and minimizing your mistakes—by correcting your errors as soon as possible, and by substituting better-performing alternatives for any underperforming investments.

CHAPTER 11

Retirement Planning

Why you should contribute as much as you can—
legally and financially—to a qualified retirement plan

QUALIFIED RETIREMENT PLAN BASICS

Probably the most common reason why people start long-term financial planning and investing is to secure a comfortable retirement. Many of the investment instruments we've discussed so far can be incorporated in a qualified retirement plan for just this purpose.

A qualified retirement plan allows people with earned income (money received as a salary, tip, bonus, or commission) to shelter part of their earnings from current taxation. The most common types of plans include IRAs, Keoghs, pension plans, 401(k)s, 403(b)s, and profit-sharing plans. The amount you can contribute, and write off, depends upon what type of plan you have and the limitations put on it by your employer. These plans are called "qualified" because they meet IRS requirements—adherence to these guidelines is what makes the contributions (investments) tax deductible and the growth and/or income tax-deferred.

Compound Interest

Just a few years before his death, Albert Einstein was asked what he considered to be the most amazing thing he had ever seen. His response was simply, "Compound interest." I believe he made this comment because the effects of compound interest, given enough time, are truly amazing. Here is a simple example that shows what Dr. Einstein was referring to.

Imagine for a moment that you are 20 years old, do not make much money, and do not expect to make a lot of money in the future. However, you do have three things working in your favor: (1) You can save $2,000 a year for the next five years. (2) You have access to some compound interest and mortality tables. (3) You are patient. For the sake of our example, assume that the $2,000 invested in each of five years averages, and continues to average until retirement, a return of 12% a year—which is what the S & P 500 has averaged over the past half century.

If you invested just $2,000 a year into an IRA for only five years you would end up with $1,181,000 when you retired at age 65. If you were married and your spouse did the same thing, as a couple you would end up with twice as much—or $2,362,000. Finally, if you each invested $2,000 every year until retirement, you would end up with $6,085,000!

Contribute What You Can Afford

There are actually some sources that say you should not contribute to any kind of qualified retirement plan. These writers argue that qualified plans cannot take advantage of long-term capital gains, and that if an emergency need for the cash in the plan does arise, the 10% penalty for withdrawals taken before age 59½, plus the payment of regular income taxes, can more than wipe out the benefits of the plan. It is obvious that none of these commentators have taken a good look at the compound interest tables or life expectancy charts. The truth is, unless you are certain you are going to inherit a sizable sum before you retire—or have some of the worst luck in the world—you must have a retirement account!

There are four reasons why you should contribute as much as you can afford to a qualified retirement plan:

1. Money compounds much faster and more frequently if it is not subject to taxation each year.
2. More compounding means you can take advantage of the big doublings that occur many years down the road (for example, when $400,000 doubles to $800,000).
3. No one can effectively predict how much money he or she will need during retirement, since there may be unforeseen medical operations, lawsuits, or divorces along the way.
4. As you get older, your career choices become narrower and your ability to save for retirement may be curtailed.

Types of Plans

How your plan works depends upon what type of plan(s) you have. All such plans have in common the following features:

1. You must be working in order to make a contribution. (You can be retired and still have a plan, but you can no longer make contributions.)
2. Contributions made by you, or on your behalf, are usually tax deductible.
3. Your earnings inside the plan grow tax-deferred (tax-free in the case of a Roth IRA).
4. No taxes are due until money is taken out of the account.
5. Money can be transferred from one account (or employer) to another without triggering a tax event.
6. Money taken out before a certain age, normally 59½, is subject to an IRS penalty and/or income taxes.
7. You can have multiple accounts, but the aggregate contribution(s) must not exceed prescribed limits.
8. The contributions can be invested in most types of investments, except for collectibles—currently U.S. minted gold and silver coins are the only exception—most types of options, and direct ownership of real estate (or anything that is considered self-dealing); other limitations may be those imposed by the plan itself.

Individual Retirement Accounts. IRAs are for anyone under age 70½. You can contribute up to $2,000 (up to $2,000 per spouse if either or both spouses are working per calendar year. Everyone who is currently working and under age 70½ can make such a contribution, which will grow tax deferred; the only question is whether or not the contribution is tax deductible.

Keogh. These plans are for people who are self-employed or work for someone who is not incorporated. There are two types of Keogh plans: profit-sharing and defined contribution. Profit-sharing plans allow you to contribute and deduct anywhere from 0% to 15% of your net earned income (income after business expenses); the percentage can be changed each year. Defined contribution plans allow contributions of up to 25% of net earned income. (In this case the formula is complex but works out to a maximum of about 21%.) Once a percentage figure is chosen (1% to 25%), it cannot be later changed unless the plan is terminated. Hybrid plans (part profit-sharing for the flexibility and part defined contribution to take advantage of the higher maximum contribution) are also allowed.

Corporate Plans. Pension and profit-sharing plans, also referred to as corporate plans, work the same way as the two types of Keogh plans already described. The percentage figure and investment choices are determined by the employer. Some corporate plans offer employees choices of one or more investments from a list; other plans do not give employees any options.

403(b). Also known as TSAs, these plans are for teachers, school administrators and staff, hospital personnel, and anyone who works for a nonprofit organization. As with a corporate plan, you cannot contribute to a 403(b) plan unless it has been set up by the corporation. In short, you cannot force your employer to start any kind of retirement plan. People eligible for TSAs may contribute up to 15% of their salary each year.

401(k). These plans are a type of corporate retirement plan. Unlike pension or profit-sharing plans, which require contributions only from the employer, 401(k) plans allow both the employee and the employer to make contributions. This type of "matching plan" lessens the corporation's burden.

ADVANTAGES OF A QUALIFIED RETIREMENT PLAN

There are three key advantages to qualified retirement plans: deductibility, deferred growth, and investment options. A deduction lowers your taxable income, which in turns lowers your income taxes. Deductible contributions lower your taxable income dollar for dollar. Once the investment is made, it grows and compounds tax-deferred. Finally, you have a wide range of investment choices, largely limited only by the employer, ranging from CDs and money market funds to stocks and bonds. A further advantage to qualified retirement accounts that is often overlooked is that some of these accounts are sheltered from creditors or legal judgments. More importantly, such accounts are "sheltered" from investors' temptations to tap it themselves—to buy a new car or go on a trip. Such "forced savings plans" can help protect you from yourself.

DISADVANTAGES OF A QUALIFIED RETIREMENT PLAN

The first disadvantage of a retirement plan is that the investments may not grow at the rate you expect. The difference between a 7% compound growth rate and 12% over 20 to 30 years can be tens or hundreds of thousands of dollars. The second disadvantage is that contributions to certain types of retirement plans may not be fully or even partially deductible. It all depends on the type of plan(s) you have and the level of your income (and that of your spouse). Third, the investment choices offered by your employer may not suit your personal investment "comfort zone."

Finally, if you need to take money out prematurely, it will most likely be subject to an IRS penalty along with income taxes.

RISK AND RETURN

The track record of retirement accounts depends on the investment(s) chosen. For the most part, Americans have selected very conservative investments for retirement accounts—bank CDs, fixed-rate annuities, and government securities. The track records of these investments do not improve just because they are part of a retirement program.

There are only two risks associated with retirement accounts—early withdrawals and poor investment choices. Early withdrawals (taken before age 59½) can be subject to a 10% IRS penalty along with income taxes. So, if you are faced with a financial emergency, you may have to give up the benefits of tax-deferred growth. The following example shows how the benefits of deferred growth can be wiped out by these penalties.

An Example

Suppose there are two investors, X and Y; both people have $10,000 to invest—and each expects a compound annual return of 12%. Investor X decides to set up a qualified retirement plan and is able to invest the entire $10,000 in a profit-sharing plan. Over the next five years, the portfolio grows at 12% a year, tax-deferred. At the end of five years, an emergency arises, and he or she is forced to liquidate the entire account. Prior to liquidation the account was worth $17,623 ($10,000 growing at a rate of 12% for five years). After the account is closed down, the figures look like this: $17,623 minus $1,762 (the 10% IRS penalty) minus $4,934 (assuming a 28% tax bracket, the taxes due on $17,623) equals $10,926. In short, over a five-year period, due to the penalty and taxes, the original $10,000 has a net growth of $926.

Investor Y decides to invest his or her $10,000 in the same investment, but not as part of a qualified retirement plan. A 12% growth rate for someone in a 28% tax bracket nets out to a 8.64% return on an after-tax basis. Over a five-year period, $10,000 growing at 8.64% compounded equals $15,134 (after taxes). At this point, it looks as if investor Y, who did not use a tax-sheltered retirement account, has come out ahead of investor X, who did set up a qualified retirement plan, by $4,208 ($15,134 minus $10,926). However, this is not the case.

Investor X was able to deduct his contributions, whereas Y could not. A $10,000 deduction for someone in the 28% tax bracket equals a $2,800 savings on federal income tax. By taking $2,800 (the tax savings) and investing it in an investment with an after-tax return of 8.64%, the money grows to $4,237 at the end of five years. Since $4,237 is a greater than $4,208 (which was investor Y's advantage), setting up a qualified retirement plan still makes sense, assuming that you don't touch the money for at least five years. (Investor Y does gain an edge if the same scenario is played out over four years or less and/or if you assume a pretax rate of return of less than 12%.)

Of much greater concern, assuming that you don't touch your retirement money for at least a few years, is how the money is invested. Qualified retirement plans are not immune from bad investments. The only difference is that you can't write off your losses in a retirement account. (Of course, your gains are not currently taxed, either.)

One of the common misconceptions about retirement plans is that they have a set rate of return. In most cases, the yield or return within a qualified retirement plan depends upon how and where the money is invested. In most cases, the employee (you) has to make choices about where the money should go.

BUYING AND SELLING WITHIN YOUR QUALIFIED RETIREMENT PLAN

Trading within your retirement plan works pretty much the same as for a regular account. Other than the issue of taxes, the only difference is that Congress and the IRS do not allow you to invest in self-dealing enterprises (direct ownership of real estate, an interest in a business you control or partially own, and so forth) or most forms of collectibles (rare coins, stamps, baseball cards, gold bullion, paintings, and so on). And, as previously mentioned, your company's plan may try to simplify administrative costs and time by further limiting your investment choices.

In the case of retirement plans you control directly, such as IRAs, Roth IRAs, and other plans, or if you are given wide latitude by your employer, trades are often handled directly between you and an investment advisor. There are no real special procedures or forms to fill out.

You track the performance of a retirement account the same way you track any other investment. If one or more of the assets you have chosen are not publicly traded, contact your employee benefits coordinator or your contact at the investment company. One of both of these people should be able to get you current prices.

TAX CONSIDERATIONS

The tax benefits are the best feature of qualified retirement plans. No other investment allows you to both write off your contribution and then watch it grow without having to pay any current income taxes.

To fully appreciate the benefits of tax-deferred growth (or income), assume that a $10,000 investment has been compounding over a 24-year period at 12% (and assume a 33% state and federal tax bracket). At the end of 24 years, a $10,000 tax-deferred investment is worth $160,000; after paying taxes (and canceling out the initial benefit of writing off the investment), the investment is worth $110,000. The same $10,000 growing at the same 12% rate, but being taxed at a 33% state and federal income tax rate each year, is worth only $80,000 at the end of 24 years. This $30,000 difference ($110,000 minus $80,000) is fully attributable to the value of tax deferral. Both investments are taxed—one is taxed each year; the other is fully taxed as money is paid out of the plan.

Limits and Qualifications

For married couples filing a joint return, IRA contributions are not deductible if the contributing spouse is not covered by another qualified plan and the couple's Adjusted Gross Income (AGI) is over $160,000. If the married spouse is an active participant of a plan, then the contributing spouse will not receive an IRA deduction (but may still contribute) if the couple's AGI is over $63,000. For a married couple filing separate returns, the figure drops to $43,000. Finally, IRA contributions made by either or both spouses is fully deductible if neither spouse is an active participant in a qualified retirement plan, regardless of AGI. Following the aforementioned restrictions, deductibility is the lesser of 100% of net earned income or $2,000.

Profit-sharing plan contributions, whether part of a corporate plan or a Keogh, are deductible for up to 15% of net earned income or $35,000, whichever is less. In the case of defined benefit plans, the formula is the lesser of up to 25% of net earned income or $35,000; the same limits apply to 401(k) plans. For those who have access to a 403(b) plan through work, the annual cap for contributions is $10,500.

You can have more than one retirement plan, but the contribution limits are not increased. It may be desirable to have more than one plan depending upon how much each plan allows you to contribute and/or the investment choices it offers.

For most plans, withdrawals made prior to age 59½ are subject to a 10% IRS penalty. This penalty can be avoided if you are over 59½, disabled, or dead (your heirs would avoid any penalty). The penalty may also be waived if the money is used for educational purposes or up to $10,000 for a first-time home purchase. Furthermore, the IRS considers any such withdrawals to be ordinary income that is fully taxable as income (similar to getting a bonus at work) for the calendar year in which the money is received.

ARE QUALIFIED RETIREMENT PLANS RIGHT FOR YOU?

I recommend participation in a qualified retirement plan to anyone who qualifies. There is nothing quite like an investment in which you get to deduct your contribution (just like a business expense or mortgage interest), watch it grow tax-deferred, and then later take the money out pretty much as you need it.

Qualified retirement plans are good choices for investors at all ages and at all risk levels. The greater your rate of return (which presumably translates into a higher risk level), the greater the benefit of tax deferral.

But, as mentioned, you can be as conservative as you want to be with the invested money. Younger investors may wish to set aside less each year than an older individual or couple who have a more stable income and who already own a house, furnishings, automobiles, and so forth.

One of the beauties of many retirement plans is the flexibility that goes along with the tax benefits. You can decide how much you invest each year and where the money is to be invested (subject to the plan's investment options). Here are some considerations when deciding which of the instruments discussed in this book to invest in as part of a qualified retirement plan.

CDs and Retirement Plans

Certificates of deposit are not usually an option within a retirement plan. However, since a large percentage of money market funds often have a modest or high percentage of their assets in CDs, you can participate in this investment somewhat indirectly.

Money Market Funds and Retirement Plans

Chances are that your qualified retirement account will include a money market portfolio as an option, either as part of a mutual fund group, variable annuity family, or variable life account. A money market account is a great place to be when stocks and bonds are declining or when you are uncertain about where retirement dollars should be invested. However, like bank CDs, this investment should not be considered a place to park money for more than a year or two—under most conditions, the period should be limited to several months or less.

Stocks and Retirement Plans

There are a few different ways in which you may be able to participate in common stocks within a retirement plan: through direct ownership, mutual funds, variable annuities, and variable life insurance. Most companies use either mutual funds or annuities for their retirement plan. The advantage of having your retirement plan in common stocks is that this will most likely be the best-performing part of the portfolio, particularly if a comparison is made after five or more years. In fact, there is a better than 50-50 chance that a stock portfolio will do better than a bond or money market account after one year. The disadvantage is that common stocks are a good way to take advantage of the capital gains tax—something you lose inside a qualified retirement plan.

In general, a moderate or very large percentage of your retirement plans should be in stocks. They have an excellent track record, and since most people cannot touch retirement accounts for a number of years, one of the greatest downfalls of stock investors—moving money around too quickly—is somewhat minimized. A case can be made against common stocks, just as a case can be made against any investment; however, one would be bucking a track record that has been unmatched for well over 100 years.

Fixed-Rate Annuities and Retirement Plans

A number of companies allow their employees to contribute retirement money only into an annuity. Fixed-rate annuities are not particularly exciting, but their return is guaranteed. If this is your only choice, you may still be able to select one or more different maturities. Since no one knows what interest rates will do next week, much less next quarter or year, in the long run you will be better off opting for an annuity whose rate is guaranteed for a few years (similar to buying intermediate-term bonds).

If your company allows you to choose between a fixed and variable annuity, chances are you will fare better, or much better, in a variable annuity that allows you to select one or more different stock and bond subaccounts.

Since money in all annuities grows and compounds tax-deferred, given the choice, you should use annuities for nonretirement accounts. There is no benefit to be gained by putting a shelter (annuities) inside a shelter (a qualified retirement plan). Moreover, annuities are more costly to administer than mutual funds, in which, given the choice, you would probably fare better.

Bonds and Retirement Plans

If you are going to own government, agency, or corporate bonds, you will want to own them inside a qualified retirement plan so that the interest payments are sheltered from current taxation. Income-oriented investors, such as retirees, can obtain a higher level of current income by going into equity-oriented mutual funds, such as growth, growth and income, or utilities funds, and setting up a systematic withdrawal plan (SWP) so that they receive monthly income that is higher than what they would get with a quality bond and still enjoy appreciation of principal (which would help offset the future effects of inflation) over the long term. Additionally, liquidations after the first year would be subject to the more favorable capital gains tax rates.

However, never make municipal bonds part of a qualified retirement plan. Everything that is in a Keogh, a pension plan, a profit-sharing plan, or an IRA is fully taxable when it is withdrawn (taken out by you). A Roth IRA is the only qualified plan where withdrawals are tax-free (contibutions to a Roth IRA are not deductible). The IRS does not, and will not, make a distinction just because you did not know any better. In fact, the only thing that is not taxed when it is withdrawn from a retirement account by you or your beneficiary(ies) is that portion that is considered a "return of after-tax dollars" (contributions that were not deductible when they went in). However, only a small percentage of retirees are affected by this situation.

CHAPTER 12

Working with Professional Help

What your broker should ask you before touching your nest egg

HOW TO SELECT A BROKER

I don't know about you, but if I need a new car, I don't just walk down the street and buy an automobile from the first dealership I come across. Similarly, I am usually not convinced by a newspaper or television ad. If I need a new doctor, or mechanic, or if I am making a major purchase, I start by asking my friends who or what they like and what their experiences have been.

It always surprises me how willing some people are to pick an individual or company to manage their investments based on a single seminar, a recommendation from a friend, or even a television advertisement. These are often the same people who have spent years worrying about how to accumulate enough in their savings to warrant professional guidance!

Just like shopping for a new appliance or baby-sitter, you need to do a little research before you hire someone or make a purchase. If you are willing to take some time and effort when buying your next stereo or television, you should also ask some questions before you hire someone to manage your investments. After all, what's more important, a $15 toaster or your financial future?

The selection process described in this section may take you a few hours to complete. At times it may seem like an inconvenience. But ask yourself, "How long did it take me to earn the money I'm ready to invest?"

What is a Broker?

A broker is someone who receives a fee or commission from a client in return for buying or selling a security or piece of real estate for that client. A broker must have a license before he or she can conduct any such transaction.

Getting a license entails studying for and successfully passing an exam. Some broker or agent exams can be passed with as little as 25 hours of preparation. Other licenses, such as those that involve the selling of stocks, bonds, limited partnerships, and REITs, take over three months of intensive study, followed by a six-hour exam.

The fact that advisors or brokers have passed a test or exam does not mean that they are completely knowledgeable in all investment areas. It simply means that they have learned the basics of their field—the competence of a successful broker comes with time.

Six Questions You Must Ask a Broker Before Investing

Most first-time callers or visitors to a brokerage firm are greeted by the receptionist, who, unless you ask for a specific broker by name, will put you in touch with the "broker of the day." At most firms, the broker of the day is assigned from a pool of available brokers, which is usually made up of brokers-in-training, relatively new recruits, or a mix of both seasoned and inexperienced advisors. By talking to the broker of the day, you are playing a form of Russian roulette with your investments.

The broker you end up talking to under these circumstances could be either extremely sophisticated or totally lacking in experience and expertise. In order to protect yourself from getting poor or dangerous advice, it is important that you ask the broker you are introduced to these six questions:

1. How long have you been a broker?
2. What areas do you specialize in?
3. What areas are you weakest in?
4. How do you stay abreast of new investment opportunities?
5. What kind of formal training or education have you had?
6. What financial groups or organizations do you belong to?

How they answer will determine whether you should accept them as your broker—or try to find someone with more experience or training. Their answer to each of these questions is important. The following section shows the reasoning behind each one of the questions.

How long have you been a broker?

This question helps you find out how much experience the broker has. After all, if you were to go in for surgery, you wouldn't want to hear your surgeon saying, "This is my first chance to operate!" You don't want someone "learning about investing" with your money.

You should deal only with a broker who has at least five years' experience as a broker. The learning curve in the brokerage business is steep, but fortunately quite a bit can be learned in five years. With this much experience, the broker has seen good and bad markets come and go. He or she has also seen how certain programs promoted by the parent firm have turned out. And the broker has also seen the results of all of the "hot tips" overheard during the past years.

Where is your expertise weakest?

Each stockbroker has certain kinds of investments that he or she is particularly interested in. Just as lawyers tend to specialize in one or two areas of the law, registered representatives develop expertise with a limited range of investment opportunities. After all, there are thousands of different stocks and bonds, not to mention the large number of convertible and preferred securities. On top of traditional stocks and bonds, there are over 10,000 different mutual funds. Add to this the several dozen current limited partnership offerings, real estate investment trusts, options, commodities, and so forth, and you have a tremendous number of investment choices. No broker can be expected to keep fully abreast of even one or two dozen different stocks and bonds!

By asking brokers about their strengths, you can see if those strengths match the areas that you are interested in. Brokers may be brilliant, with lots of experience, but if they specialize in commodities and you are interested in mutual funds, they are not right for you.

Where is your expertise the weakest?

We all have strengths and weaknesses. By pointing out his weaknesses, the broker is showing you that he is being honest. More importantly, you now know the areas in which you shouldn't rely on the broker for advice.

It is likely that your broker knows other brokers who are experts in those areas he or she is weakest in. He or she can always help you find advisors who specialize in those areas—who can help coordinate your overall game plan.

How do you stay abreast of new investment opportunities?

One of the best reasons for using a stockbroker is that he or she should not only keep track of your investments, but also be constantly learning about new investments and techniques that can help better serve your needs. There is no reason to pay a commission to a broker who knows only as much as or less than you do about an investment. Seek out someone who is constantly looking at new opportunities, whether these opportunities are in the area of specific investments, financial planning, estate planning, or income tax reduction.

Find out what periodicals, newsletters, and other research sources the registered representative reads regularly. A good broker does not confine his or her research to in-house reports that may or may not be biased.

Last, but not least, by seeing how brokers stay up to date, you can get a sense of whether or not they view the business as a way of making commissions or as a profession in which they can learn something new every day. A love of knowledge usually indicates a broker with an edge over his or her peers—which can translate into more profit in your portfolio.

What kind of formal training or education have you had?

When a brokerage firm hires a registered representative, its chief concern is whether or not the person will be good at sales. Knowledge of investment products is not considered important since trainees will learn about products during their orientation. In the financial services industry, "good at sales" means that the person is generating a lot of fees or commissions for the firm. This is in direct conflict with your interests.

Ask the broker what his or her educational background is. Extensive training and education not only shows dedication and a certain degree of intelligence, it is also usually an indication of someone who will truly try to serve the client's needs.

The majority of brokers and agents cannot claim any of the designations in the following list. This doesn't mean that they are incompetent. It simply means that they have not taken the time or incurred the expense of going through a formal training program. It is also quite common to meet with a designated advisor who is not a broker. This kind of advisor typically prepares a financial plan or other investment summary and is compensated at an hourly rate, by retainer, or with a flat fee. The most popular designations in the brokerage community include the following:

1. *CFP (Certified Financial Planner):* This designation is received after an advisor completes a six-part, two-year-long program. The graduate ends up with a great breadth of knowledge of investment products and strategies. There are approximately 35,000 CFPs in the nation—a small number compared to all those who call themselves "financial planners."

2. *CLU (Chartered Life Underwriter):* This is the highest designation one can obtain in the life insurance industry. It requires a ten-part program that takes approximately four years to complete. The graduate ends up with a strong grounding in the different aspects of life insurance and estate planning. This designation has been around for over 60 years.

3. *ChFC (Chartered Financial Consultant):* This is the insurance industry's answer to the financial planning designation, or CFP. It involves a ten-part program that takes approximately two to three years

to complete. Graduates end up with a wide range of investment knowledge, with an emphasis in the area of insurance products.

4. *CFS (Certified Fund Specialist):* This designation is granted after the advisor completes a 60-hour program that leads to the only designation in the area of mutual funds. Graduates have an extensive knowledge of mutual funds, how to match client objectives with specific funds, and modern portfolio theory (MPT), and have a strong overview of financial and estate planning. There are fewer than 5,000 CFS graduates.

5. *Board Certified:* This is the upper echelon of the investment and financial planning world. Successful graduates must have several years of experience, obtain client endorsements, pass a comprehensive exam, and have a thorough financial plan scrutinized by a board of examiners.

All these designations require continuing education. This ongoing learning process helps ensure that the advisor is constantly exposed to new ideas, concepts, and products that may improve the advice they give you as an investor. In addition, all these designations are based on current information that is both practical and topical. Formal degrees, with their emphasis on theory and abstract concepts, are less important. Nonetheless, undergraduate and graduate degrees are a definite plus if the degrees are earned in areas that relate to financial services. A Ph.D. in history is of no value to a client looking for a fixed-income specialist. However, an MBA graduate who took some investment classes could be an excellent choice as an advisor.

What financial groups or organizations do you belong to?

I have been attending financial planning seminars and broker conventions for close to 20 years; I still walk away from each of them with at least one good idea that will benefit my clients. We are never too old or too smart to learn from others.

Sharing information with your peers is a great way to learn about new and unique strategies or approaches in the investment industry. New, practical information and new ideas should translate into better performance for both the broker and his or her clients. During your interview with the prospective broker, find out how he or she exchanges new ideas with other brokers.

If your prospective broker can successfully answer these questions, move on to the next section. If he or she cannot, move on and start the process with another broker. There are tens of thousands of stockbrokers out there; most of them would like to have your business. Never forget how much time and effort it took you to save the money you are now thinking about investing.

HOW TO SELECT A FINANCIAL PLANNER

Choosing the right financial planner can have a great impact on your financial future. This person may end up introducing you to investments you had never previously considered, and to strategies for reducing risk that make achieving your goals that much more certain. It is hoped that the planner can add a sense of objectivity to your investment process that you may not have.

Selecting a financial planner is not that much different from selecting a broker. However, since you will be working much more closely with a financial planner, there are two areas that need special attention: the planner's background and references.

A financial planner is like a coach on a team. He or she is expected to know quite a bit about a range of different strategies and options. Your financial planner may end up being not only your central money manager, but also the one who puts your retirement plan into effect. Therefore, his or her skills and experience as a broker are also important.

Most financial planners are not experts in every aspect of investments, insurance, taxes, and estate planning. But they should at least have a good grounding in each of these areas and perhaps be specialists in one or two. They should also admit to their weaknesses in those areas that they are not particularly strong in, and demonstrate that they have access to one or more experts in those areas. If necessary, these outside experts can be brought in to coordinate and implement a specific part of your financial plan.

The financial planner you are considering should be able to give you a list of references. Contact two or three of these references and ask whether or not they are satisfied with their experience. You will get a good sense as to the planner's knowledge, attention, and sensitivity to his or her clients.

As with stockbrokers, you should interview at least two or three financial planners. Pay particular attention to their educational and work history. You want to work with someone who has the experience you lack—someone who has spent years educating himself or herself in financial planning, and who continues to keep abreast of new developments in the profession.

WORKING WITH AN INSURANCE AGENT

Your insurance agent should help you with insurance products—and only insurance products. Most insurance agents are not trained in handling securities. They may possess good estate planning skills, but usually fall short in the area of financial planning. If you are going to use an insurance agent or broker in areas other than risk transference or estate planning, interview that person the same way you would a financial planner or stockbroker.

Ideally, the agent you end up using should represent a number of different insurance carriers. If you have access to products from a range of companies, you should end up with competitively priced policies.

Your decisions about insurance should be based on three things: quality, price, and service. Make sure the company that insures you is rated highly by the A. M. Best Company; only deal with companies rated either A, A+, or A++. The ratings represent the two highest ratings from this neutral source. As an added precaution, seek out companies that are also highly rated by another outside rating service, such as Moody's or Standard & Poor's.

Since there are approximately 2,500 insurance companies in the United States, there is also quite a bit of competition. In addition to shopping for quality, shop for the best price. You will be surprised to see the difference in premium payments for the identical coverage from quality insurers.

TAXES AND YOUR ACCOUNTANT

The accountant, tax preparer, or enrolled agent who prepares your taxes can end up saving you hundreds, if not thousands, of dollars. You can invest these dollars, which would normally have gone to Uncle Sam, and turn them into a larger nest egg at retirement. The person who prepares your taxes can also give you ideas on how to minimize your taxes in future years.

When interviewing prospective tax preparers, narrow your search to those who match your needs. That is, you do not need a CPA who is also a tax attorney to prepare a simple return. On the opposite end of the spectrum, you shouldn't use a "quickie tax preparer" if you have multiple business interests or properties.

Get price quotes from two or three accountants that fit your needs. Good accountants are worth their weight in gold. The savings they generate can easily offset your tax preparation bill.

Do not use an accountant to make your investments, unless that person also possesses additional degrees or, better yet, designations in the areas of investments, financial planning, or insurance. Keeping abreast of the Internal Revenue Code (IRC) is more than a full-time job. Expecting your tax preparer to know the ins and outs of the IRC and be a whiz about stocks and bonds is ridiculous. It makes as much sense to ask your stockbroker to prepare your taxes.

Once you have gone through the interviewing process, you can sit back and relax. It is hoped that you can assemble a talented team that is on your side—a group of professionals concerned about your well-being, and not the fees or commissions they can earn. The time you invest in evaluating your investment advisors should pay off in financial security and personal satisfaction.

ADDITIONAL INFORMATION

For a list of financial planners or advisors in your area, contact one of the organizations listed here.

If you are thinking of doing business with a securities firm that you are not familiar with, check it out in advance. The National Association of Securities Dealers (NASD) (301-590-6500) and the Securities Investor Protection Corporation (SIPC) (202-371-8300) are good sources of information about their member firms.

You should also verify your broker's history. State security regulators keep track of brokers registered to sell securities in individual states and whether they have any past violations. The North American Securities Administrators Association (202-737-0900) can tell you how to contact the securities commission in your state. The NASD can also provide information about past violations by brokers.

The Institute of Business and Finance
7911 Herschel Avenue, Suite 201
La Jolla, CA 92037
(800) 748-5552

The Institute of Certified Financial Planners
7600 East Eastman Avenue, Suite 301
Denver, CO 80231
(800) 282-7526

The National Association of Personal Financial Advisors
1130 Lake Cook Road, Suite 105
Buffalo Grove, IL 60089
(800) 366-2732

The American Institute of Certified Public Accountants
Personal Financial Planning Division
1211 Avenue of the Americas
New York, NY 10036

Appendix

FINANCIAL PLANNING CHECKLISTS

The financial planning checklists that follow will help you review the major financial planning issues that you face. Whenever your answer is no, make a note to yourself so that you are sure to follow up and complete the task.

PLANNING AND RECORD KEEPING

1. Have you established realistic short-term financial goals?
   YES ❑   NO ❑

2. Have you established realistic long-term financial goals?
   YES ❑   NO ❑

3. Have you developed a satisfactory record-keeping system that is simple enough to use yet comprehensive enough to be useful?
   YES ❑   NO ❑

4. Do you use a safe deposit box for storage of valuable papers and possessions?
   YES ❑   NO ❑

5. Do you maintain an up-to-date inventory of the contents of your safe deposit box?
   YES ❑   NO ❑

6. Have you prepared a comprehensive and up-to-date inventory of household furnishings and possessions?
   YES ❑   NO ❑

7. Do you prepare a personal balance sheet periodically?
   YES ❑   NO ❑

8. Have you prepared a household budget, listing expected income and expenses?
   YES ❑   NO ❑

9. Do you have sufficient cash reserves to avoid being financially strapped periodically because of unexpected expenses or large annual bills?
   YES ❑   NO ❑

INSURANCE

1. Have you obtained sufficient life insurance to prevent your dependents from suffering financial hardship in the event of your death?
   YES ❑   NO ❑

2. Has your spouse obtained sufficient life insurance to meet the financial needs of dependents in the event of his or her death?

    YES ❏   NO ❏

3. Have you determined the most appropriate form of life insurance to meet those needs?

    YES ❏   NO ❏

4. Does the entire family have comprehensive and continuous health insurance coverage?

    YES ❏   NO ❏

5. Have any elderly members of the family acquired Medicare gap insurance and considered acquiring long-term care insurance?

    YES ❏   NO ❏

6. Do you have adequate long-term disability insurance coverage (equivalent to at least 60% of your salary)?

    YES ❏   NO ❏

7. Does your spouse have adequate long-term disability insurance coverage?

    YES ❏   NO ❏

8. Do both spouses' have disability policies that provide benefits as long as they are prevented from gainful employment in their "usual and customary" occupation?

    YES ❏   NO ❏

9. Do your disability policies cover both illness and accident?

    YES ❏   NO ❏

10. Do you have adequate homeowner's or renter's insurance?

    YES ❏   NO ❏

11. Does your homeowner's or renter's policy provide replacement cost coverage for the home?

    YES ❏   NO ❏

12. Does your homeowner's or renter's policy provide replacement cost coverage for the contents of the home?

    YES ❑   NO ❑

13. Have you obtained additional insurance protection for jewelry, silverware, safe deposit box contents, or other valuables?

    YES ❑   NO ❑

14. Do you have adequate personal liability (umbrella) insurance coverage?

    YES ❑   NO ❑

15. If your profession warrants it, do you have adequate professional liability insurance coverage?

    YES ❑   NO ❑

16. Does your spouse have adequate professional liability insurance coverage, if applicable?

    YES ❑   NO ❑

BORROWING AND CREDIT

1. Have you established your credit through borrowing for worthwhile purposes?

    YES ❑   NO ❑

2. If you have a home equity loan, are you paying off the principal on a regular basis?

    YES ❑   NO ❑

3. Are you confident that you will have sufficient resources to fund your children's education?

    YES ❑   NO ❑

4. Are you aware of your personal credit rating as reported by the national credit bureaus?

    YES ❑   NO ❑

5. If you have an automobile loan, will it be paid off well in advance of your acquiring another automobile?

    YES ❑   NO ❑

SAVINGS AND INVESTMENTS

1. Do you save through payroll withholding or other savings programs?
   YES ❑   NO ❑

2. Have you established an emergency fund of liquid savings equal to at least three months salary?
   YES ❑   NO ❑

3. Is more than two-thirds of your total portfolio invested in the stock market?
   YES ❑   NO ❑

4. Is more than two-thirds of your total portfolio invested in savings instruments (for example, savings accounts, certificates of deposit, bonds, and government securities)?
   YES ❑   NO ❑

5. Do you have appropriate investment objectives?
   YES ❑   NO ❑

6. Are your investments appropriate for your age, wealth, and family status, as well as for your investment objectives?
   YES ❑   NO ❑

7. Do you review your investment portfolio regularly?
   YES ❑   NO ❑

8. Are your investments appropriate in terms of risk?
   YES ❑   NO ❑

9. Do you participate in your employer's stock purchase and/or thrift plans?
   YES ❑   NO ❑

10. Is your investment portfolio appropriately diversified?
    YES ❑   NO ❑

11. If you expect to receive a substantial inheritance, have you considered how to invest and manage it?
    YES ❑   NO ❑

REAL ESTATE

1. If you don't own a home or condominium, do you plan to buy one in the future?

    YES ❑   NO ❑

2. If you are contemplating future real estate investments, either directly owned or through limited partnerships, do you understand the risks associated with them?

    YES ❑   NO ❑

3. Are your real estate investments appropriate to your financial circumstances?

    YES ❑   NO ❑

TAX PLANNING

1. Are you well informed about tax-saving techniques and current tax law?

    YES ❑   NO ❑

2. Do you keep a notebook handy to record miscellaneous tax-deductible expenses?

    YES ❑   NO ❑

3. Do you maintain adequate tax records?

    YES ❑   NO ❑

4. Are you familiar with tax-advantaged investments?

    YES ❑   NO ❑

RETIREMENT PLANNING

1. Do you make regular contributions to an Individual Retirement Account?

    YES ❑   NO ❑

2. If you have any income from self-employment, do you contribute to a Keogh Plan or Simplified Employee Pension (SEP)?

    YES ❑   NO ❑

3. Are you currently enrolled in a company pension plan?

    YES ❑   NO ❑

4. Do you participate in an employer-sponsored salary reduction plan?

YES ❏ NO ❏

5. If you are contemplating early retirement, are you preparing for the increased financial requirements of such an action?

YES ❏ NO ❏

6. Will your estimated retirement income be sufficient to meet your retirement expenses?

YES ❏ NO ❏

7. Are you taking action now to ensure financial security by retirement age?

YES ❏ NO ❏

8. If you are nearing retirement age, have you evaluated your investment portfolio mix in light of retirement income needs?

YES ❏ NO ❏

9. If you are nearing retirement age, have you decided where to live during your retirement?

YES ❏ NO ❏

10. If you are nearing retirement age, have you discussed expected pension benefits with a company representative?

YES ❏ NO ❏

11. Have you requested a record of your earnings and an estimate of your retirement benefits from the Social Security Administration?

YES ❏ NO ❏

ESTATE PLANNING

1. Do you have a valid will?

YES ❏ NO ❏

2. Do you review your will periodically to ensure that it still conforms to your wishes?

YES ❏ NO ❏

3. Does your spouse also have a valid and current will?
    YES ❑   NO ❑

4. Have you prepared a letter of instructions?
    YES ❑   NO ❑

5. Has your spouse prepared a letter of instructions?
    YES ❑   NO ❑

6. Have you discussed both the location and the contents of the will and letter of instructions with your family?
    YES ❑   NO ❑

7. Have you appointed a financial guardian for any dependent children?
    YES ❑   NO ❑

8. Have you appointed a personal guardian for any dependent children?
    YES ❑   NO ❑

9. Have you established an adult guardianship arrangement (durable power of attorney, living trust) in the event that either spouse becomes disabled or mentally incapacitated?
    YES ❑   NO ❑

10. Is the manner in which you own property (single ownership, joint ownership) consistent with effective estate planning?
    YES ❑   NO ❑

11. Have you evaluated the estate planning and estate tax implications of owning business or real estate interests in more than one state?
    YES ❑   NO ❑

12. Have you evaluated the impact of possible long-term uninsured hospitalization during your retirement?
    YES ❑   NO ❑

Index

About the Author

Gordon K. Williamson, JD, MBA, MS, CFS, CLU, ChFC, RP, is one of the most highly trained investment counselors in the United States. Williamson, a former tax attorney, is a Certified Financial Planner and branch manager of a national brokerage firm. He has been admitted to The Registry of Financial Practitioners, the highest honor one can attain as a financial planner. He holds the two highest designations in the life insurance industry, Chartered Life Underwriter and Chartered Financial Consultant. He is also a real estate broker with an MBA in real estate.

Mr. Williamson is the founder and executive director of the Institute of Business and Finance, professional education programs that lead to the designations "CFS" and "Board Certified" (for more information, call 800-848-2029).

He is also the author of 32 books, including *The 100 Best Annuities You Can Buy, The 401(k) Book, All About Annuities, How You Can Survive and Prosper in the Clinton Years, Investment Strategies Under Clinton/Gore, The Longman Investment Companion, Investment Strategies, Survey of Financial Planning, Tax Shelters, Advanced Investment Vehicles and Techniques, Your Living Trust, Sooner Than You Think*, and *Low-Risk Investing*. He has been the financial editor of various magazines and newspapers and a stock market consultant for a television station.

Mr. Williamson directs an investment advisory firm located in La Jolla, California. The firm specializes in financial planning for individuals and institutions ($100,000 minimum account size). Additional information can be obtained by phoning 800-748-5552 or 858-454-3938.

fastread
Personal Finance

Understand managing, saving, and investing money!

Trade paperback, $5.95
ISBN: 1-58062-510-X

Face it, most people's lives revolve around money. Money has a significant impact on your lifestyle, your feelings of security, and sometimes even your state of mind. But you don't have to become a slave to it. **fastread** Personal Finance is a quick, easy guide to help master all financial affairs.

Inside readers will discover:
- How to create, calculate, and maintain a personal budget
- The truth about credit cards and how to take advantage of their benefits while avoiding their traps
- How to defeat debt
- How to plan for long-term financial security
- And much more!

fastread Personal Finance is designed to offer a practical method to managing, maintaining, and increasing the money you have. From budgeting to investing to preparing tax returns, this book is perfect for those wishing to take command of their present and future financial status.